THE VIRUS INVADERS

THE
VIRUS INVADERS

ALAN E. NOURSE, M.D.

FRANKLIN WATTS
NEW YORK—LONDON—TORONTO—SYDNEY
A VENTURE BOOK

Illustrations by Vantage Art

Photographs copyright ©: The Bettmann Archive: pp. 11, 15, 58; Photo
Researchers, Inc./Science Photo Library: pp. 13, 56 (both CNRI), 23 (Dr.
Jeremy Burgess), 27 (Will & Deni McIntyre), 32 (David M. Phillips/
Population Council), 37 (Dr. Arthur Lesk), 43, 44 (both Charles Dauquet/
Institut Pasteur), 76 (George Leavens), 87 (Philippe Plailly); Custom Medical
Stock Photo: pp. 16 (Weybridge/SPL), 17 (CNRI/SPL), 77; Phototake: p. 22.

Library of Congress Cataloging-in-Publication Data

Nourse, Alan Edward.
The virus invaders / Alan E. Nourse
p.   cm.—(A Venture book)
Includes bibliographical references and index.
Summary: Explores different viruses and our body's defenses
against them.
ISBN 0-531-12511-4
1. Viruses—Juvenile literature.   2. Virus diseases—Juvenile
literature.   [1. Viruses.   2. Virus diseases.]   I. Title.
QR365.N67   1992
616'.0194—dc20   91-36650 CIP AC

CONTENTS

THE VIRUS INVADERS

AN ANCIENT FOE

Sometimes medical miracles occur in mysterious ways. Here's one example:

All you know is that you're suddenly very sick. You didn't feel good after dinner last night, and you woke up at midnight with chills and a fever. At 4:00 A.M. you were in the bathroom vomiting, and you had the great-grandfather of all headaches. A few hours later you had a dry, hacking cough and felt short of breath. Every muscle and bone in your body ached, and by evening you thought you were going to die. By the next morning you half-wished you would, just to get it over with.

If you saw your doctor, he'd say you had the flu and you'd feel worse before you felt better. Nothing to do but go back to bed, drink lots of fluids, and be sure not to take any aspirin.* No medical miracles from *him*. But then, after a few more days, things begin to change. You

*When there's any possibility of flu or chicken pox, children and young people should never take aspirin. An uncommon but dangerous complication known as *Reye's syndrome* could result. An alternative drug known as *acetaminophen* (Datril or Tylenol) can be used instead to relieve headache and muscle aches.

start feeling better. The muscle aches and headache go away. So do the coughing and shortness of breath. You feel totally exhausted, but you begin to think maybe you *will* survive after all.

In fact, a real medical miracle is taking place inside your body without a bit of help from you or your doctor. All by itself, your own built-in *immune system* is fighting a vicious attack by a dangerous virus invader—and winning! In a few more days you will be on your feet again. What's more, that particular virus invader won't be able to invade your body again for months or even years—because your immune system won't let it.

A LANDMARK EXPERIMENT

Sometimes medical miracles occur by even more mysterious means, including sheer blind chance. Consider what happened in the small town of Gloucestershire in England almost two hundred years ago.

It was in the year 1796 that an obscure country doctor in that little town put his professional reputation—and the life of a young patient—at terrible risk by performing a startling and dangerous experiment.

First, the doctor made two small incisions on the arm of his patient, a healthy eight-year-old boy named James Phipps. Next, he took some infected pus from a sore on a local milkmaid's hand and rubbed it into the boy's wound. As the doctor expected, the boy soon developed a sore there on his arm just like the milkmaid's—a minor infection that soon healed.

But six weeks later the doctor took a second, much more dangerous step. This time he took infected matter from a sore on the arm of a victim of *smallpox*, one of the most dreaded and deadly diseases known, and rubbed it into new scratches he had made on James Phipps's arm. By all rights, that boy should have been overcome by smallpox within a few days. But nothing of the sort happened. The boy didn't even get slightly sick. A medical

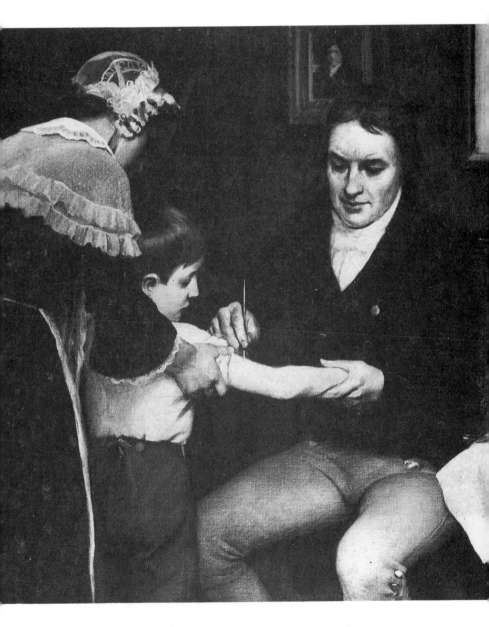

*Dr. Edward Jenner (1749–1823) performing
the first vaccination on eight-year-old
James Phipps on May 14, 1796*

miracle had occurred. That country doctor, Edward Jenner, had discovered a safe and sure means of preventing a terrible epidemic disease, and young James Phipps remained safe from smallpox for the rest of his life. Almost exactly 180 years later, in 1976, that dreadful disease was finally wiped out altogether. Not one single case has occurred anywhere in the world since that time.

Today the very thought of performing an experiment like Jenner's would make a modern doctor's blood run cold. Edward Jenner literally didn't know what he was doing. He didn't have any idea what caused smallpox. He didn't have any idea why infected material from a milkmaid's cowpox sore would prevent it—or even that it actually might. His experiment was based on a totally unproven old wives' tale that milkmaids who had had cowpox never got smallpox. Nobody today would dream of testing an unproven vaccine first on a human being and then exposing that person to a deadly disease to see if the vaccine worked. But that was exactly what Jenner did!

The crowning irony was that Jenner's experiment worked by sheer blind chance alone. Cowpox and smallpox are caused by two different viruses. A vaccine against one virus will virtually never protect a person against a different virus. It just happened that the cowpox virus and the smallpox virus were so very similar, in certain ways, that a rare "crossover" protection occurred—and James Phipps lived his life free of smallpox.

ANOTHER MEDICAL MIRACLE

Ninety years after Edward Jenner stumbled on his smallpox vaccination, Louis Pasteur, the great French chemist and medical scientist, conducted an equally risky experiment. But this time things were a bit different. The patient was already infected with a deadly disease and would have died if Pasteur had not decided on a dangerous intervention.

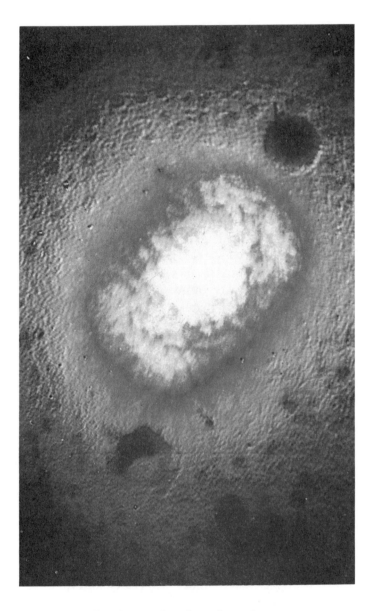

This photo, taken through an electron microscope, shows a single virus particle of the pox virus family of viruses. The family includes the viruses that cause smallpox and cowpox.

By the early 1880s Pasteur was already a world-renowned microbe hunter. He was a champion of the so-called *germ theory of disease*, the notion that all infectious and communicable diseases were caused by tiny living microorganisms, or "germs," passed from one person to another. A number of disease-causing *bacteria* (one kind of germ) had already been identified. Pasteur himself had been studying rabies, a deadly disease passed to humans by the bite of an infected dog. Once symptoms of this disease appeared in an infected human, the victim invariably died a horrible death. Pasteur believed that rabies, like other infections, must be caused by some kind of bacterium. He had also found that if he transferred bits of infected nervous tissue from one laboratory animal to another, the infected tissue's power to cause fatal rabies seemed to grow weaker and weaker.

Pasteur suspected that an extract made from such weakened, or *attenuated*, infective material might be injected into a person as protection from the deadly symptoms of rabies even after that person had been bitten and infected—but such an extract had never been tested on a human being. Then in 1885 young Joseph Meister, badly bitten by a rabid dog, was brought to Pasteur's laboratory. Pasteur injected the boy with his weakened rabies extract, and as week followed week the boy remained free of rabies. (In fact, the boy lived until 1940.) Pasteur's rabies vaccine had worked another medical miracle, and it became the standard treatment for people bitten by rabid dogs.

Pasteur knew more about what he was doing than Jenner did, but he couldn't seem to locate the actual germ that caused rabies. Possibly, he thought, it was just too small to be seen easily under a microscope. He had no way of knowing then that rabies is caused by a *virus*, an infective agent so very tiny that it could not possibly have been seen at all, even with the best microscopes available at the time.

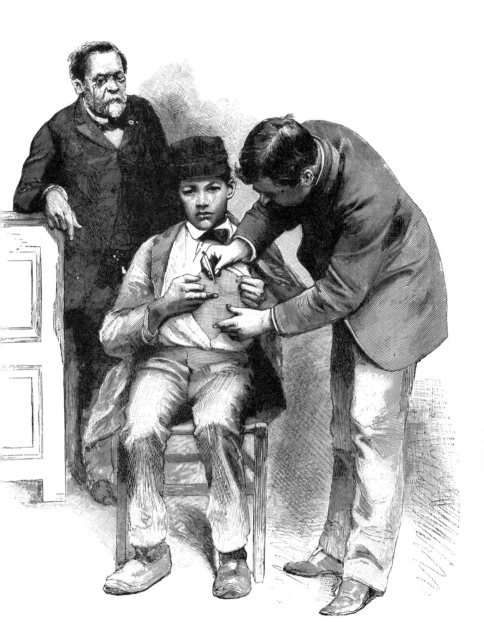

Louis Pasteur supervising vaccinations
at the Pasteur Institute in Paris

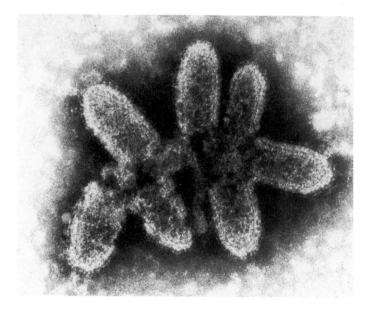

An electron micrograph of particles of the rabies virus. Rabies is an acute and often fatal disease of the central nervous system.

AN ANCIENT FOE

Today we think of Jenner and Pasteur as pioneers fighting a battle against a silent, invisible foe they could neither see nor understand. But humankind had been suffering from virus-caused epidemics since long before recorded history. The Great Red Plague that Thucydides described in his account of the ancient war between Athens and Sparta in 431 B.C. may have been nothing more than a terrible epidemic of rubeola, or red measles—still a familiar virus infection today. The mummified remains of ancient Egyptian nobility have shown deformities characteristic of paralytic poliomyelitis (infantile paralysis), another dreaded viral disease.

A row of virus particles of the influenza virus buds from the surface of an infected cell. Spikes projecting from the envelope surrounding the viruses are used as a way to attach the virus to receptors on the surface of the host cells.

Smallpox was a widespread killer in Europe from the Middle Ages on. When American soldiers and pioneers moved across the Great Plains in the early 1880s, the smallpox they brought with them took more Indian lives than all the Indian wars put together. The Indians had never encountered smallpox and had no natural defenses against it. Yellow fever, still another viral disease, struck repeatedly in the eastern coastal cities of America in the late 1700s, culminating in a fearful epidemic in Philadelphia in 1793. More recently, a worldwide epidemic of virus-caused influenza in 1918 and 1919 afflicted as many as half a billion people and contributed to the death of some ten million. What is more, we now know that viruses are responsible for such children's diseases as chicken pox, rubella (German measles), and mumps, as well as infections ranging all the way from minor head colds and fever blisters to such dangerous killer diseases as hepatitis B and AIDS.

Viruses are very important in our everyday lives. We have been engaged in a mortal struggle against these infective agents for as long as we've been around, and we have not yet won that battle. And today, when certain viruses have found ways to manipulate or destroy our best natural defense against them—our immune systems—our very survival on earth is in danger, for we can't survive for very long without healthy immune systems working for us.

Everybody today needs to be well acquainted with these virus invaders and with our defenses against them, for our own protection—and in some cases, for survival. That is the purpose of this book.

TRACKING DOWN THE VIRUS INVADERS

It's not surprising that a great medical pioneer like Louis Pasteur didn't know what a virus was. For all our long contact with viral infections, it has only been within the past fifty years that medical researchers have really begun to understand what these disease-causing entities are, how they behave, and—above all—how they invade living cells to cause such a multitude of diseases.

THE ELUSIVE INVADERS

Why did viruses remain shrouded in mystery for so long? As early as the mid-1600s scientists were becoming aware that the world is populated with multitudes of tiny living organisms, so very small they can be seen only with the aid of a microscope. Two hundred years later Louis Pasteur proved for the first time that certain of these tiny organisms, by then known as bacteria, caused certain infectious diseases. Between 1850 and 1900 many infectious bacteria were identified for the first time. The bacteria that caused tuberculosis, the streptococcus organisms that caused scarlet fever, and the staphylococci responsible for pimples and boils were all discovered through painstaking research. Still smaller microbes, the *rickettsia*, were found to cause typhus fever and Rocky Mountain spotted fever. Certain single-cell animal-like organisms called *protozoans* were shown to cause such diseases as malaria and African sleeping sickness.

All these tiny organisms could be seen under the microscope. Almost all of them would grow and reproduce themselves in the laboratory. All of them behaved very much like any other living cells, including the cells that make up the human body. It seemed more and more likely that they might cause *all* infectious diseases.

But in some of the most deadly infections—smallpox, rabies, and yellow fever, for example—no such microbes could be found. Whatever caused these infections had to be something different from the known bacteria. Pinning it down, however, was a baffling problem. How could you track down something you could neither see nor understand, something so tiny and elusive that you couldn't even be sure it existed at all? Even after these tiny tyrants had finally been identified, it took decades of tedious laboratory work to learn what they really were and how they might be conquered.

THE EARLIEST CLUES

One reason the early study of viruses was so difficult was that researchers did not know what they were looking for. It seemed natural to assume, as Pasteur did, that the microbes which caused rabies, smallpox, and yellow fever were just ordinary bacteria that were too small to be seen. And when the first clue to the real truth was uncovered in 1892, hardly anyone even noticed it.

The man responsible was an obscure Russian researcher named Dmitri Ivanovski, and he was not studying human diseases at all. His concern was the *tobacco mosaic disease*, a plant disease that caused the mottling and destruction of tobacco leaves. It was known that on contact the sap of an infected tobacco plant could quickly infect a healthy plant. Searching for the bacterium that might be responsible, Ivanovski crushed infected tobacco leaves in sterile water and then passed the water through an earthenware filter with pores so tiny that even the smallest known bacterium would be trapped. To his chagrin, however, the infective agent he was seeking passed right through; the clear, filtered solution still retained its power to infect tobacco leaves even after it had been filtered again and again.

Ivanovski published a report of his odd findings, but it received little attention. He didn't even believe it himself; he thought something was wrong with his filters. Then, six years later, the same experiments were done independently by a Dutch botanist named Martinus Willem Biejerinck. Like Ivanovski, Beijerinck found that the infective agent, whatever its nature, remained in the filtered extract and could infect healthy tobacco plants even after many filtrations. What was more, plants infected with this fluid could infect healthy plants, which could then infect still other healthy plants, and so on. Whatever the infective agent was, it seemed to grow and multiply. Yet the infectious capacity of this fluid could easily be destroyed simply by heating it.

In 1898 Beijerinck published his studies and drew an odd conclusion. The infective agent, he decided, wasn't a microbe at all. It was something quite different, some totally new disease-causing agent that existed in a fluid state. He called it a *contagium vivum fluidum*, a "contagious living fluid." Later he applied the name *virus*, from a Latin word meaning "poison," to describe such an agent.

Other investigators soon began discovering similar "filterable" disease agents. In 1898 Friedrich Loeffler and Paul Frosch proved that hoof-and-mouth disease, an extremely contagious infection of cattle, was caused by such an agent. In 1901 Walter Reed and a team of American scientists showed that yellow fever was also transmitted by a *contagious fluid*. As dozens of other diseases were traced to these strange, elusive entities, they became known as *filterable viruses*.

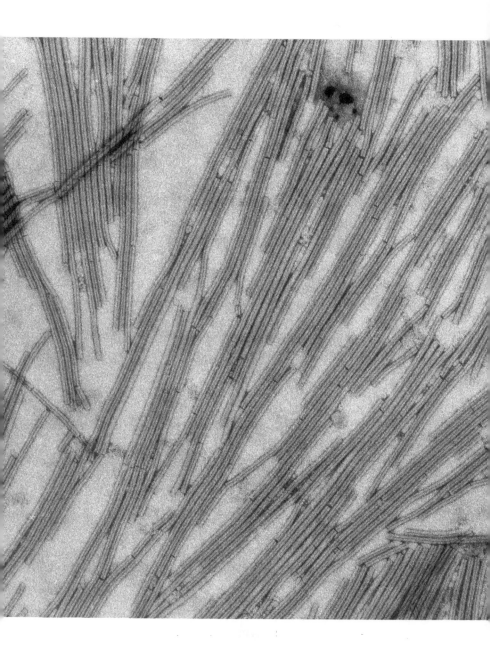

An electron micrograph of particles of the rabies virus. Rabies is an acute and often fatal disease of the central nervous system.

WHAT WERE THEY?

Despite this flurry of discovery, however, the same baffling question remained: what *were* these new disease agents? Virus hunters knew virtually nothing about them. And there seemed to be no way to study them directly, the way disease-causing bacteria had been studied. Except for one or two so-called great viruses, which could be seen as hazy blobs at the very outer limit of microscopic magnification, the newly discovered viruses were simply too tiny to be seen at all. Some researchers wondered if viruses might be as small as individual protein molecules. And although they appeared to multiply, none of them could be made to grow or reproduce in the laboratory as bacteria did.

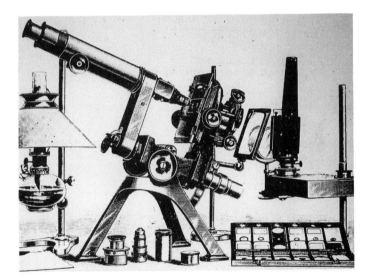

An engraving of the Powell & Lealand No. 1 single lens microscope built around the midnineteenth century. It was considered one of the best microscopes ever made and was in use, with modifications, until the twentieth century.

In the long run, it was necessary to devise a whole new series of laboratory techniques in order to learn anything at all about these elusive entities. As a first step, investigators began refining and improving the filters they used.

In 1931 an American scientist named W. J. Elford made filters from collodion, a porous plasticlike material that had previously been used to keep bacteria out by coating wounds. Elford's collodion filters had pores of known graded sizes. With them he was able to sort out viruses of different sizes, from comparatively large ones that were held back even by large-pore filters, to exceedingly tiny ones that would pass through even the finest pores.

This, of course, demonstrated clearly that viruses were not liquid in nature. They were, in fact, different-size particles suspended in the filtrates, and it was those particles that were infective, not the fluid. Elford showed that each of a number of known viruses had its own characteristic size. Some, such as the vaccinia virus that caused cowpox, were comparatively huge, almost as big as the smallest known bacteria. The rabies virus was only about half as big. Others were only one tenth or one twentieth the size of the vaccinia virus, while still others were so much smaller they could easily pass through the finest filters Elford could create.

Other workers found that the ordinary laboratory centrifuge could help tell one virus from another. Each different virus had its own characteristic weight as well as size, so the heavier viruses sank to the bottom of the centrifuge tube faster than the lighter ones. The virus of influenza was first identified by this method. And out of these studies still another important fact emerged: each of the known disease-causing viruses seemed to cause just one specific disease—that it, a given virus of identifiable size and weight always caused just one disease and no other.

THE STRUCTURE OF VIRUSES

All this still didn't reveal what viruses *were*. So in the early 1930s virus hunters turned to chemical analysis to learn more about them. At that time a number of biochemists had been studying an odd class of natural body chemicals known as *enzymes*. These substances seemed to speed up a wide variety of chemical reactions in the body that were vital to life but tended to progress very slowly without the enzymes' help. But what was the chemical makeup of these substances? Chemists soon answered that question by chemically crystallizing a number of enzymes and proving that they were simply special protein molecules.

These studies stirred the curiosity of an American biochemist named Wendell M. Stanley. If enzymes were proteins that could by crystallized in pure form, what about viruses? He began studying the old familiar tobacco mosaic virus to try to determine its chemical makeup. After isolating it in purified form, Stanley subjected the virus itself to chemical analysis to determine its characteristic chemical components. And in 1935 he finally ended up with some fine needlelike crystals that had all the infectiveness of the virus. The crystals proved to be a kind of chemical compound known as *nucleoprotein*.

Other workers analyzed other viruses, and gradually this tedious, unromantic laboratory work began to pay dividends. It was found that *all* viruses were nucleoproteins—a combination of two kinds of biochemical constituents, proteins and *nucleic acids*. Beyond this, however, viruses seemed to differ widely one from another. Some seemed to consist of a single tiny bundle of nucleic acid surrounded by a protein coating and nothing more. Others, especially the larger viruses, also contained carbohydrate molecules, fatty material, copper or sodium salts, enzymes, and even vitamins, together with their basic proteins and nucleic acids. These complex viruses seemed far more like ordinary bacteria than their tinier, simpler cousins. But were they truly living organisms? An enzyme was clearly not a living substance; it was just a chemical compound, period. But even the tiniest virus seemed to reproduce itself within its host cells, one basic thing that a nonliving chemical compound could *not* do.

SEEING THE VIRUS AT LAST

Researchers still had no way to guess what viruses looked like or how their nucleic acid–protein parts were put together. Then, around 1940, a special kind of microscope opened a whole new avenue of virus research.

Ordinary light microscopes failed to reveal most viruses for a very simple reason: the viruses were considerably smaller than the average wavelength of visible light. Bacteria could be seen under regular microscopes because light waves passing them would strike them and cast a shadow that could be focused into a sharp image. But viruses were so tiny they could, in effect, hide between the light waves. What was needed was a microscope that used some form of "light" with a much shorter wavelength than visible light.

So what about using a stream of electrons—tiny negatively charged elementary particles with marked wavelength qualities—instead of visible light in a new kind of microscope? In 1932 the German electrical engineer Ernst Ruska built a crude *electron microscope* that could magnify about 400 times. By 1937 James Hiller, a Canadian physicist, had constructed a much-refined instrument that could magnify some 7,000 times, three times the magnification of the best light microscope. Later, electron microscopes were developed that could magnify more than 100,000 times—and at last virus particles could actually be seen!

The electron microscope worked very much like an ordinary light microscope with a few key modifications.

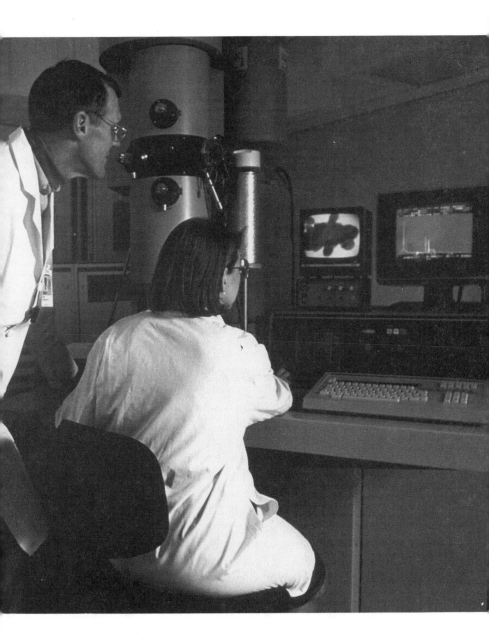

*An up-to-date electron microscope through
which even the tiniest of virus particles can be seen*

Instead of a beam of light, a beam of electrons was sent through a long hollow tube to strike a sample of virus-containing material. Electrons striking this sample were scattered every which way, but the unscattered electrons could be focused with electromagnets onto a fluorescent screen at the end of the tube. And there, like magic, clear images of the long-sought virus particles could be seen, magnified between 40,000 and 100,000 times.

THE QUARRY TRAPPED

With the help of the electron microscope, virus researchers in the 1930s and 1940s at last began to make real progress. With clear photographs showing viruses of many shapes and sizes, and with laboratory analyses that showed them basically to be nucleoproteins, scientists no longer had any doubt that these elusive infective entities indeed existed.

But were they living organisms? In some ways, it certainly *seemed* that they were. They somehow could get inside living host cells through cell membranes that ought to have kept foreign materials out. And once inside their host cells, viruses multiplied. True, they could manage this only with the aid, and at the expense, of the host cells, which were usually killed in the process. But overall, viruses displayed at least *some* lifelike characteristics.

The question was, *how* did they reproduce? In 1955 a German-American biochemist named Heinz Fraenkel-Conrat made a key discovery. By carefully separating the nucleic acid portion of a virus from the protein part, he found that it was only the nucleic acid part of the virus that caused infection. The protein part was as dead and lifeless as any other chemical. It was the nucleic acid part alone, inside the host cell, that seemed to force the host cell to manufacture not only more virus nucleic acid molecules but more of the virus's protein coatings as well. The virus's nucleic acid seemed to carry a code message instructing the host cell to make perfect duplicate virus particles.

Today that code message is known as the *genetic code*.

From the very beginning, virus research had been time-consuming, tedious, and not very romantic. But with the aid of electron microscopy, tissue-culturing techniques, and a growing understanding of the genetic code and how it works, virologists have learned more and more about the nature and behavior of many viruses. In the next chapter we'll see where our understanding of viruses stands today.

THE NOT-QUITE-LIVING ENEMY

What do we know about viruses today?

First of all, for big troublemakers, viruses are very tiny. While small bacteria like the streptococci are approximately one micron in diameter (that is, about 4/100,000 of an inch), the very largest viruses known today are only about one-third that size, and many viruses are as much as thirty-five times smaller. Some are less than *one-millionth* of an inch in diameter—so tiny most of us can't even imagine how small they are!

Tiny as they are, viruses come in a wide variety of sizes and shapes. Some appear fluffy, like cotton balls. Others are long, thin rods. Still others look like many-sided crystals. One type of virus resembles a six-sided bullet, while another looks like a rolling pin with one handle missing. Others, all bristling with spikes, look like nothing so much as the deadly floating mines used to blow up battleships.

All told, more than 1,400 different kinds of viruses are now known, and many can invade the human body. Some are transmitted in the air, others in droplets of moisture from the sneezes and coughs of infected persons. Still others are carried in food or water contaminated by infected human waste, while others are spread by having sex or by coming in contact with an infected person's blood.

Other viruses are harmless to human beings, but attack other life forms. Many attack only plants. Dogs can be infected by deadly distemper viruses or parvoviruses that leave human beings untouched. But other viruses attack many different species with equal ease. The rabies virus, deadly to humans, is also deadly to dogs, cats, coyotes, skunks, raccoons, even bats. And yellow fever cannot be wiped off the face of the earth, as smallpox has been, because that virus infection is also present in wild monkeys in various inaccessible tropical areas of the world.

Viruses can enter our bodies through virtually any break in the skin, or through various moist mucous membranes—membranes lining the nasal passages, the respiratory tract, the intestine, and the lining of the eye. Viruses that cause genital herpes, hepatitis B, and AIDS can invade directly through the moist linings of the sex organs. Most infective viruses have their own preferred route of entry. Wherever they may enter, viruses can cause a multitude of different human infections. And not a single virus has yet been found to be helpful in any way, in contrast to the many bacteria that perform useful tasks within the body. Viruses are totally parasitic; they take what they need and give nothing in return.

DEAD OR ALIVE?

Today we know that viruses are startlingly different from any of the disease-causing bacteria. Bacteria are clearly living cells. They need water or some other kind of solvent in order to survive. They need oxygen from some source. They need food—nutrients of some sort. They grow, within limits. They produce their own energy, and they reproduce themselves by cellular division. Some can even move around.

Viruses need none of these things and can do none of

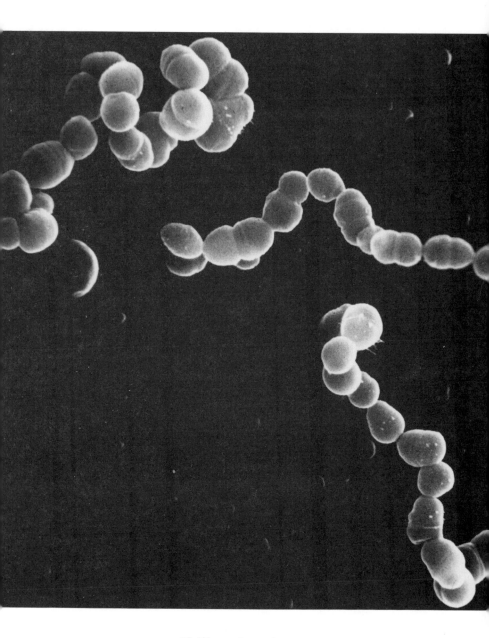

*Unlike a virus, the streptococcus
bacteria is a living cell.*

these things by themselves. They don't need any food. They don't need water or any other solvent. They don't need oxygen either. In fact, there are only two things they really *do* need. They need the right temperature, because if they get too hot, they will be destroyed. And they need to be free from noxious chemicals, such as formaldehyde, and from radiation, either of which can also destroy them.

Given those two requirements, however, viruses don't actually need to do *anything*. They can just sit there forever. In fact, they *can't* do anything by themselves. They can't grow. They can't reproduce themselves. They don't produce energy or carry on any ordinary life processes of their own. They can't do anything at all—*until they get inside a living cell*. When we say that all viruses known today are totally parasitic, we mean that they can "live" and reproduce only inside the living cells of some susceptible host—for instance, in the lung cells of a mouse; in the cells of a chick embryo still growing in its shell; or in the cells of the nasal passages, the blood or the bone marrow, the liver, the intestine, or the brain of a human being or some other living organism. Isolated from living cells, viruses are as lifeless as sawdust. They can do nothing but sit and wait for the right host cells to come along.

Does this mean that viruses outside living host cells are "dead"? Well, not quite, but they're not quite "living" either. Viruses are really nothing but inert little bundles of possibilities until they get inside living host cells. Outside such cells, those possibilities are never realized and nothing happens. Inside such cells, the possibilities are released and all sorts of things can happen.

Most viruses are remarkably hardy. They do not "die," as many bacteria do, when deprived of nutrients or water. They can remain in their inert but potentially dangerous state of "suspended animation" for months or years, possibly for centuries. Even freezing may not bother them. There may well be inactive viruses surviving on specks of dust in outer space, totally unharmed and unchanged, for ages on end—we just don't know.

Finally, only a few viruses seem to be affected in the slightest by antibioticlike drugs that can destroy so many of the disease-causing bacteria. Antibiotics work by fouling up the metabolic processes of the bacteria. Most viruses don't have any metabolic processes for such drugs to foul up.

The truth is that viruses are not really living cells at all, by any ordinary definition. They contain no protoplasm, the semifluid life substance that fills most living cells. Some of them are so completely unlifelike that they can actually be crystallized in pure form in the laboratory, as lifeless and harmless as salt in a shaker—until they come in contact with susceptible living host cells. But they *do* possess one power that sets them far apart from any other disease-causing microbe. Although they can't themselves perform the sort of vital life functions of which even the lowliest bacteria are capable, viruses have the amazing capacity *to force the living cells of their hosts to perform those life functions for them.* And herein lie the "possibilities" we spoke of earlier—the viruses' "secret of life" and their deadly danger as well.

HOW NORMAL CELLS FUNCTION

So far we've said quite a bit about what viruses are *not*. Then what *are* they, and how can they force living host cells to obey their commands? To understand this, we need to understand a bit about how perfectly normal cells go about their business.

Nucleic acids in one form or another make up the remarkable genetic, or hereditary, material found in the nuclei of all living cells. Tiny packets of nucleic acids called *genes* are strung together to form structures called *chromosomes* in the cell nuclei. There are forty-six chromosomes in every normal human cell nucleus. These con-

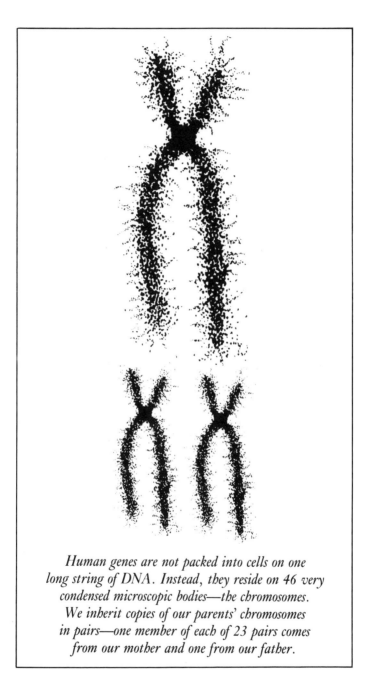

Human genes are not packed into cells on one long string of DNA. Instead, they reside on 46 very condensed microscopic bodies—the chromosomes. We inherit copies of our parents' chromosomes in pairs—one member of each of 23 pairs comes from our mother and one from our father.

sist of twenty-two pairs of very similar chromosomes. Of the twenty-third pair (which determines a person's sex), one half is very similar to the rest and is called the X chromosome. The other half may be a similar X chromosome or a runty little thing called a Y chromosome. A combination of two X chromosomes produces a female, but a combination of an X chromosome and a Y chromosome produces a male.

It is these packets of nucleic acids on the chromosomes that make it possible for normal cells to manufacture proteins, enzymes, energy, and heat, and to perform dozens of other functions necessary for life. These packets of nucleic acids also enable cells to reproduce themselves and pass on their characteristics to new generations of cells.

If we could look at these chromosomes more and more closely, we would see that they are really tangled packets of special nucleic acid molecules known as DNA (short for *d*eoxyribo*n*ucleic *a*cid). DNA molecules act as special *master molecules*, controlling all of the cell's many vital life functions. They are shaped in the form of a double spiral strand, or *double helix*, much like the framework of a spiral staircase with connecting stairs, or *bases*, made of protein building blocks known as *amino acids*.

GETTING THE MESSAGE TO THE CELL

One major way in which DNA molecules can control a cell's vital life functions is by directing the activities of another form of nucleic acid in the cell's nucleus. This form of nucleic acid is known as RNA (for *r*ibo*n*ucleic *a*cid). RNA molecules seem very similar to small fragments of DNA molecules, except that they have just a single spiral strand, connected to different amino acid bases, much like a broken or incomplete section of a spiral staircase.

Through their special arrangement of amino acid

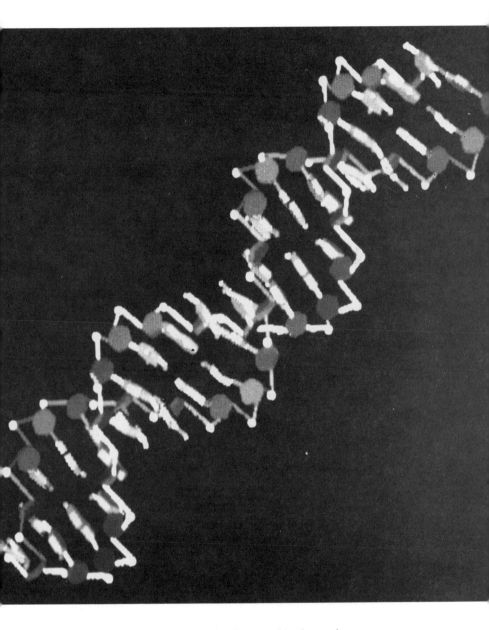

*A computer molecular graphic shows the
structure of the DNA double helix.*

bases, DNA fragments contain coded messages, like recipes, to direct the cell in how to make certain proteins and other vital substances. These "recipes" are called genes. Such a gene is comparable to Grandma's recipe card for making her special molasses brownies. To save space and to help keep them secret, Grandma wrote her recipes in her own special shorthand code. Before we can make those molasses brownies or anything else from one of Grandma's recipes, we have to decode Grandma's shorthand. First, a rough copy of the DNA's gene (Grandma's recipe) is decoded and written onto a single-stranded piece of RNA. This is called *transcription*. During this process a certain amount of useless recipe information (like the last line of Grandma's last recipe or the beginning of the next) gets thrown out. The result is a *messenger* form of RNA, actually nothing more than a very accurate, perfect, readable recipe card for Grandma's special molasses brownies.

At this point the messenger RNA for the brownies then leaves the cell's nucleus and moves out to other parts of the cell where good things are made—to the "kitchen," we might say—and passes the message on to the cooks for making Grandma's brownies. And lo and behold, the cell has soon manufactured an ample supply of perfect, absolutely scrumptious Grandma's special molasses brownies. Scientists would then say that the molasses brownie gene has been "expressed," or has done its job.

Of course there aren't any genes, or "recipes," for Grandma's molasses brownies anywhere in the body. But there *are* genes for directing the manufacture of just the right special proteins and enzymes, and for shaping things correctly, and for creating heat and energy in the cell. These gene "recipes" are passed on to the cell very similarly to the way our imaginary "molasses brownie" gene is passed on from the master DNA molecules through RNA messengers into the cell, where they are expressed, and the vital needs of the healthy, living cell are satisfied.

ENTER THE VIRUS—NATURE'S TINIEST TYRANT

The things we've talked about are things that happen in a normal living cell all the time, as long as you're alive. But as we have seen, viruses are not normal living cells. They aren't even cells at all. Viruses are just tiny bundles of DNA or RNA hereditary material—naked genes—without the living cell around them. They have been described as "chromosomes on the loose," or tiny packets of "infectious heredity,"* and their nucleic acid is the key to their power. When a susceptible cell is attacked by a virus, the DNA or RNA from the virus—very similar to that of the cell itself—pours into the cell, attaches itself to the cell's normal DNA molecules, and sets up a new "master control system" all its own, with a totally different purpose. Instead of directing the manufacture of substances useful to the cell, the viral nucleic acid forces the cell to produce enough more viral nucleic acid molecules and protein coatings to form hundreds or even thousands of new, fully formed virus particles.

This whole process can take place with breathtaking swiftness. In some cases as little as twenty-four *minutes* may elapse from the instant the virus particle first enters its cell victim until the cell bursts apart to release hundreds of new virus particles that have been formed within it. Then, with the host cell damaged or destroyed, each of the newly formed virus particles goes forth to attack another cell, and the whole process is repeated again and again, leaving behind an ever-expanding trail of dead or damaged host cells.

PATTERNS OF INFECTION

How does a virus attack a susceptible host cell? How can it tell which host cells are susceptible to invasion? And

*See Isaac Asimov, *Asimov's New Guide to Science* (New York: Basic Books, 1984), p. 672.

once it has found the right cell, how does the virus get its DNA or RNA inside in the first place? After all, living cells are surrounded by tough cell membranes designed for the specific purpose of keeping foreign materials out. Obviously, these are extremely important questions if we want to understand how virus infections come about, and especially if we're looking for ways to prevent viral invasions of host cells.

Until recently these key questions have gone unanswered. We still don't know exactly how a virus can tell which potential host cell is susceptible, or vulnerable to attack, and which isn't. But in very recent years investigators have begun to find some clues as to how the virus, once it has found a susceptible cell, gets inside.

Living cells have *portals*, or entryways, through their cell membranes so that useful molecules—nutrients and salts, for example—can get in and waste materials can get out. We now know that living cell membranes are studded with special surface molecules called *receptors* that act as potential portals. These receptors are often molecules of complex sugarlike compounds known as *polysaccharides*.

When a virus does encounter a susceptible host cell, it has to find a portal for entry. Most of the cell surface is an impenetrable barrier. But the polysaccharide receptor molecules stick out from the cell surface, and these molecules have individual three-dimensional shapes. In one recently studied case, the receptor molecules form little cigar-shaped projections that have special little bulges and grooves formed by the three-dimensional arrangement of their atoms. The protein molecules that coat the virus also have little bulges and grooves. Investigators now think that the virus particle literally bounces gently around from place to place on the cell surface, probing, so to speak, until its coating protein molecule finds a "good fit," with its bulges and grooves perfectly matching those on the receptor molecule. Once that "good fit" is found, the protein coating of the virus particle *sticks* to the cell there. An entry or portal has been found. The viral DNA or RNA moves through the cell membrane into the cell's interior. The protein coating, no longer needed, is discarded. Sometimes it just falls away outside the cell. Sometimes the whole virus, protein coating and all, is engulfed by the cell, and the protein is then destroyed, leaving the naked DNA to do its work.

Once the virus is inside the host cell nucleus, in order to force the cell to replicate virus DNA for new virus particles, or to manufacture new virus protein coatings, the genetic messages coded in the virus DNA must be transcribed onto RNA fragments. These "messenger RNA" fragments then carry their messages to the cell's protein-manufacturing areas. This is the way most viruses force the host cell to do their bidding. But a few viruses have to do it in reverse. These viruses contain their viral genetic messages encoded on RNA alone. To accomplish protein production and replication of the virus, their RNA message must first be translated into DNA. It is as though these special RNA viruses have only a shorthand code for the various ingredients of Grandma's special molasses brownies, but no amounts, and no directions for mixing the ingredients together or baking the brownies, unless they can put them together correctly into the full uncoded recipe in a segment of DNA. To make it possible for these RNA viruses to do this—to "transcribe the recipe in reverse," so to speak—these so-called *retroviruses* must have a special enzyme inside them to make this reverse transcription possible. And so they do—a special enzyme that is appropriately known as *reverse transcriptase*. One familiar example of such a retrovirus is the human immunodeficiency virus or HIV, the virus that causes AIDS.

What we've been discussing is a sort of general pattern for how a typical virus, any virus, can shoulder its way into a susceptible host cell and then force the host cell to do what the virus wants. It seems very much like brutal, aggressive shock troops invading a small neighboring country, taking over its government, and then forcing the country to do what the invader wants. Of course, this picture is fanciful. A virus can't think. It doesn't really *want* anything, strictly speaking. It simply exists the way it's made. When conditions are wrong for it, it just sits there, existing. When conditions become right, it does what it does because of the way it's made, and we speak of it as a "viral invasion," followed by reproduction or *replication*—that is, copying—of the virus particles, and later the further invasion of other host cells by those new virus particles. What *we* see as the end result of all this is a viral infection that damages our bodies, makes us sick, and may even kill us. The truly amazing thing is that we have to get down to such incredibly tiny details as the actual three-dimensional shape of individual molecules in order to see how all this can come about. It's hardly any wonder that viruses have been so very difficult to understand.

All virus invasions are not quite as blunt and straightforward as all this. In some cases, for example, the virus particles attach their nucleic acid to the DNA molecules in the host cell nucleus, but nothing seems to happen immediately. Rather than forcing the immediate replication of the virus particles, the virus nucleic acid may just remain attached to the host cell DNA and then be reproduced along with the host cell DNA each time the host cell divides. As a result, many generations of host cells may be silently infected by the original virus particle. Then later, when conditions are right, the viral nucleic acid can become active in all the affected cells at once, releasing tens of thousands of new virus particles in a single wave!

The fact that some viruses carry special "helper enzyme" molecules to help them replicate is very important—because here is one place that certain antiviral drugs *can* interfere with the reproduction of the viruses. In peo-

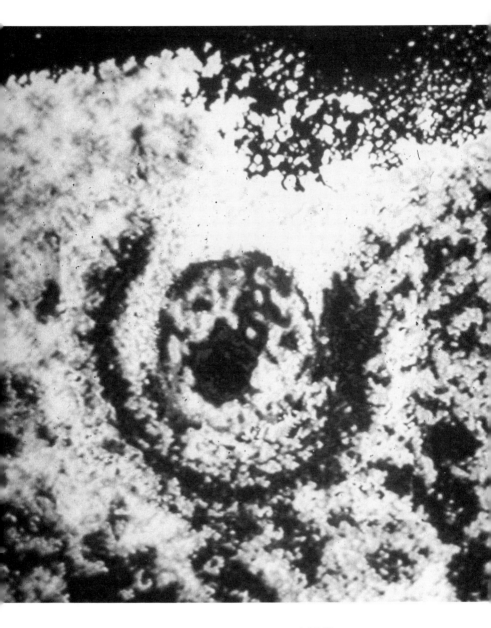

*HIV (the virus that causes AIDS)
penetrating a cell's tissue*

HIV leaving an infected lymphocyte

ple with AIDS, for instance, the drug *zidovudine*, better known as AZT, can block the function of the AIDS virus's reverse transcriptase enzyme and thus slow down the replication of the virus. Many AIDS patients taking this drug become less sick and actually live longer as a result. And there is reason to hope that AZT given very early in the HIV infection, before symptoms have appeared, may prevent the disease symptoms from developing for a long time.

VIRAL "SHAPE-CHANGERS"

Viruses have certain other characteristics that make them especially difficult to study and pin down. One is a tendency toward viral "shape-changing," or *mutation.* In some viral families, the virus that you carefully studied and identified one year isn't quite the same virus the next year; it has become something different.

This isn't really surprising when you remember that the infective portion of a virus is its nucleic acids, DNA or RNA. In 1953 James Watson and Francis Crick published their famous paper describing the actual structure of DNA molecules—the familiar double-spiral, or double-helix, shape, much like a spiral staircase with parallel spiral railings separated by "rungs," or "steps," composed of various amino acids. As studies of these molecules continued, it became clear that portions of DNA might easily be cut off and taken out, or glued together again in the wrong sequences. Since the genetic code "messages" carried by these molecules depended on the exact sequence of amino acids on the molecule, such deletions or rearrangements *changed* the genetic code and created new and different messages.

In some viruses these changes take place frequently and spontaneously. Sometimes, when a virus is replicating or duplicating its DNA, a chunk gets stuck back "wrong" by accident. Some enzymes may "cut and paste" chunks of DNA in the wrong sequence. Certain kinds of radiation disrupt the sequences and lead to different, or mutated, viruses with slightly different genetic codes. Scientists in the laboratory have found ways to delete chunks of DNA or to change their sequences on purpose. But the *natural* alterations mean that in some virus families the virus strains are constantly changing.

Take the influenza viruses, for example. When the first vaccines to protect people against flu were developed, they worked very well—the person who had flu shots didn't get flu that year. But the same vaccine didn't work so well the next year, and by the third year epidemics of flu were occurring that were completely uncontrolled by flu shots—because the virus strains had changed so much. New vaccines had to be developed to prevent infection from the mutant strains. Now each year the vaccines must be changed to cope with the mutant strains of flu virus that appeared the previous year. This is the reason we still have flu epidemics almost every year in spite of very sophisticated vaccines and the widespread use of flu shots.

Finally, some viruses exhibit another characteristic that happens to be very useful in fighting viral diseases: they undergo significant changes when transferred from one living tissue culture to another. For one reason or another, they gradually lose their disease-producing potential, becoming progressively less virulent. By using certain dangerous strains of viruses that have become weakened or attenuated (from a Latin word meaning "diluted" or "made thin") in this fashion, scientists have been able to develop vaccines that can protect people from infection by more virulent, unweakened strains of the virus.

This, of course, was exactly what Louis Pasteur had been doing with rabies-infected material when young Joseph Meister was brought to his laboratory badly bitten by a rabid dog. And it explains why the rabies virus extract Pasteur gave the boy to save his life prevented the virulent rabies virus from taking hold. The Sabin polio vaccines and some measles vaccines were also made from attenuated viruses. We'll have more to say about the development of protective vaccines in Chapter 5.

Over the years virologists have learned more and more about the nature and behavior of many viruses and about the kinds of viral diseases that have plagued humankind since before recorded history. We'll take a look at some of these diseases in the next chapter.

COMMON AND UNCOMMON VIRAL DISEASES

How many times have you come down with a scratchy throat, a headache, a little fever, a stuffy nose, and a dry cough? If you've seen a doctor, he or she has probably said, "Hard to tell, but it's probably some virus."

The chances are that your doctor was right. Virus infections are an almost everyday occurrence in our lives. A great many different varieties are recognized today. The common cold can be caused by any one of dozens of different *rhinoviruses*. A wide variety of influenzalike illnesses and respiratory tract infections, some mild, some severe, are caused by large families of *parainfluenza viruses* and *adenoviruses*, distinguishable one from another only in modern virus laboratories. In fact, so many minor respiratory and intestinal infections are caused by viruses that we don't even try to distinguish them as separate diseases. Most of them cause no more than a few hours of minor discomfort at worst, and many of them don't cause any symptoms at all!

Some viral diseases, however, are not so vague and indefinite. Some have very clear and specific recognizable signs and symptoms. Some can cause severe and prolonged illnesses, and a number of them are outright killers. But mild or dangerous, many viral infections share certain characteristics.

PATTERNS OF VIRUS INFECTION

First, viruses are characteristically spread by way of respiratory tract secretions, through contact with intestinal wastes, through contact with the bodily fluids of infected people, and through sexual contact; they gain entry into our bodies through mucous membranes.

Among those spread by way of coughing, sneezing, kissing, or just close contact in the same room are the families of rhinoviruses and parainfluenza viruses that cause the common cold, influenza, viral bronchitis, and viral pneumonia. The adenoviruses attack mucus-secreting glands in the respiratory tract or become lodged in lymph nodes scattered throughout the body.

Another large group, the so-called *enteroviruses*, attack the cells and organs of the intestinal tract and are spread by direct or indirect contact with infected people, contaminated food or water, or unwashed hands. These viruses are responsible for headaches, fever, and many cases of "summer diarrhea," or gastroenteritis (intestinal flu), as well as certain kinds of meningitis. Among the most dangerous of the enteroviruses are those that cause poliomyelitis. We don't ordinarily think of polio as an intestinal infection, but that's exactly what it is. In areas where the disease is still prevalent, most cases go unrecognized as polio because they show symptoms only of a mild diarrheal disease. Only rarely does the virus go on to attack nerve cells in the spinal cord and cause the dreaded symptoms of paralytic polio.

Other viruses can be spread either by sexual contact with an infected person or by contact with infected blood or other body fluids—for example, by sharing dirty intravenous drug needles. HIV (the AIDS virus) and the viruses that cause hepatitis B and C are the most notorious of these. And the herpesviruses that cause genital herpes are primarily spread by having sex with an infected person.

This brings up a second curious characteristic of many

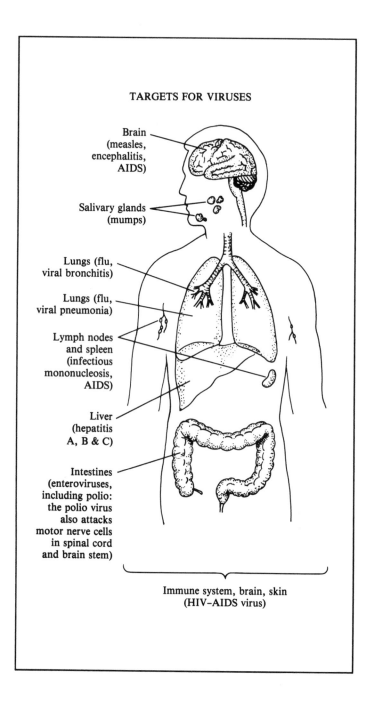

TARGETS FOR VIRUSES

Brain
(measles,
encephalitis,
AIDS)

Salivary glands
(mumps)

Lungs (flu,
viral bronchitis)

Lungs (flu,
viral pneumonia)

Lymph nodes
and spleen
(infectious
mononucleosis,
AIDS)

Liver
(hepatitis
A, B & C)

Intestines
(enteroviruses,
including polio:
the polio virus
also attacks
motor nerve cells
in spinal cord
and brain stem)

Immune system, brain, skin
(HIV–AIDS virus)

disease-producing viruses: even the most dangerous do not always produce the same severity of illness in one victim as in another. A person's general level of health and vitality may help him or her resist a viral infection. Among the best ways to avoid serious viral infections are immunization (against measles, mumps, German measles, polio, and hepatitis B, among others); avoiding contact with an infected person; and maintaining a strong, healthy body with nutritious meals, regular exercise, and adequate rest. Run-down, exhausted, or malnourished individuals fall victim most easily to viral infections. So do the very young and the elderly. And a person whose immune system has been weakened by some outside influence may be a sitting duck for certain virus infections that a normal person would shake off very easily.

SYMPTOMS AND SIGNS OF VIRAL INFECTIONS

Whether mild or severe, viral infections are often accompanied by certain characteristic signs and symptoms that differ markedly from those that signal bacterial infections. In a bacterial infection the white blood count often rises dramatically; in a viral infection it is more likely to fall *below* normal. A low-grade fever of 100° or 101° F (37.8° or 38.3° C) is more common with viral infections than the high fever so often seen with bacterial infections. Headache, nausea, and loss of appetite commonly accompany a viral infection, and the muscles and bones of the back, neck, and legs tend to ache, sometimes so severely that the victim feels as if he or she had been hit by a car or fallen down a flight of stairs.

These symptoms, together with a sense of extreme tiredness or exhaustion, make up what is known as *general malaise* (literally, "general ill-comfort"), a condition so characteristic of viral infections that doctors can often identify the problem even when no specific symptoms are present. What's more, many viral infections may leave the victim feeling totally exhausted and used up for days or weeks, sometimes even months, after the active infection and its symptoms have subsided. This recovery phase following certain viral infections can present special dangers because at these times the victim may be highly vulnerable to bacterial infections that appear in the wake of a viral infection.

In addition to such general symptoms, many viral infections cause *specific* symptoms related directly to the part of the body being attacked. A runny nose, a scratchy throat, and a tendency to sneeze or cough is characteristic of the common cold. In viral bronchitis a dry, hacking cough is common, while the victim of viral pneumonia may suffer pain and tightness in the chest, persistent deep coughing, and sometimes even shortness of breath. Nausea, vomiting, abdominal cramps, and diarrhea are typical of an enterovirus infection. In other viral infections, a characteristic skin rash may appear. Thus *rubeola* (red measles) is marked by the appearance of coarse reddish brown spots on the skin. In contrast, *rubella* (German measles, or three-day measles) causes a finer pinkish red skin rash. Chicken pox, perhaps the single most contagious viral disease known, is easily recognized by the small watery blisters that appear on the skin all over the body.

Certain other serious infections deserve special mention. Among the most troublesome are virus infections that attack cells in the liver and cause *hepatitis*, or inflammation of the liver. In *hepatitis A* (also called infectious hepatitis or viral hepatitis) the virus is spread by contaminated food or water and has caused local epidemics traced to infected food handlers. Its even more dangerous twin, *hepatitis B*, or serum hepatitis, is commonly spread by the use of dirty hypodermic syringes, by transfusions of contaminated blood, or by sexual contact. These closely related viruses plus a third one now known as *hepatitis C* (formerly called hepatitis Non-A, Non-B) all attack and destroy cells in the liver. Along with nausea and fever, victims often have severe pain in the upper right corner of the abdomen, just under the ribs. As liver cells are destroyed, the bile that is normally released into the digestive tract backs up into the bloodstream instead and causes the skin and the whites of the eyes to turn yellow, a condition known as *jaundice*.

All forms of virus-caused hepatitis are dangerous for several reasons. In a particularly severe acute attack, so much of the liver may be destroyed that the victim goes into liver failure and dies. This happens in about ten out of every one hundred cases of hepatitis B. Among those who survive hepatitis A and hepatitis B, there can be so much scarring of the liver that a long-term condition known as *cirrhosis* can occur, impairing liver function for the rest of the patient's life and sometimes causing life-threatening hemorrhages (massive intestinal bleeding) later on.

Hepatitis B and hepatitis C are particularly nasty for two other reasons. First, about a third of the victims continue to carry the live virus in their bloodstreams for years after recovery, so they are constantly at risk of infecting others. And an abnormally high percentage of these former victims of hepatitis B and hepatitis C develop cancer of the liver later on—just one of the links between viruses and cancer that we will discuss in Chapter 6.

Crowded housing and poor sanitation have led to serious epidemics of hepatitis A and hepatitis C in some of our major cities during late summer and fall. Fortunately, people who have been exposed (family members of victims, health workers, and people living in an epidemic area) can obtain temporary protection against these infections by having shots of *gamma globulin*, a portion of the blood serum that contains protective antibodies and can prevent the viruses from gaining a foothold if it is used soon enough after exposure. And in 1981 an effective vaccine against hepatitis B was finally perfected and approved by the U.S. Food and Drug Administration (FDA).

A FAMILY OF VILLAINS

Infectious mononucleosis is another common—and often very puzzling—viral infection. It's called that because a certain abnormal kind of white blood cell often appears in the bloodstream during the infection. For most victims, infectious mono is a comparatively mild disease, but its symptoms may linger for weeks—longer than most viral diseases—and some victims are disabled for months. Adolescents and young adults seem most susceptible to this infection—the offending virus is transmitted in saliva, accounting for the nickname "the kissing disease." No vaccine exists to prevent mono, but even a mild case seems to confer lasting immunity.

Today we know that several different types of infectious mononucleosis are caused by variations of the so-called Epstein-Barr virus, or EBV, discovered in 1964 by British virologists M. A. Epstein and Y. M. Barr. These viruses are members of a family of notorious troublemakers known as the *herpesviruses*. In addition to causing infectious mononucleosis, EBV can also play an important role in the development of two rare forms of human cancer—a lymph gland cancer found exclusively among natives of West Africa, and a nose-and-throat cancer occurring mainly in China.

Recently EBV has also been suspected of causing a strange new malady that seemed to appear in the late 1980s and has become widespread among young adults, the so-called *chronic fatigue syndrome*. The major sign of this illness is the development of extreme exhaustion, or fatigue, which goes on and on for months or even years, sometimes totally disabling its victims. Other symptoms include low-grade fever, headaches, muscle and joint pain, and depression. Because some victims were found to have high levels of Epstein-Barr virus antibodies in their blood, doctors at first thought this condition was some kind of chronic EB infection, but other patients showed no sign of EB antibodies. Today researchers suspect that the disorder results from some kind of virus-caused immune system disturbance in which the patient's immune system is constantly "turned on," as if continuously fighting some foreign invader that isn't even present in the body anymore.

Other members of the herpes virus family are responsible for other unpleasant and sometimes life-threatening problems. The *herpes simplex virus 1* (HSV1) causes irritating and unsightly cold sores around the lips. Its cousin, *herpes simplex virus 2* (HSV2) is responsible for genital herpes, a painful and recurring infection of the genital organs that is transmitted by sex contact and plagues a great many young people who haven't learned to protect themselves against it. And genital herpes in a newborn baby, contracted from the mother during birth, can actually cause the baby's death in severe cases.*

Herpes viruses are very skillful at evading our immune defenses and "hiding out" in the body so that, once we are infected, we never get rid of them. The herpes simplex viruses hide out in this fashion for years, so a person who gets genital herpes has the virus in his or her body forever and may have many recurrent attacks. The same is true of the *herpes zoster virus*, which causes ordinary chicken pox. This childhood disease clears up very quickly, but the zoster virus is not thrown off by our immune defenses, as other viruses are. Rather, it sneaks into nerve cells in the spinal cord and remains quietly in hiding for many years. Then, years later, it may be reactivated—no one knows quite why—and cause a painful skin infection known as *herpes zoster*, or shingles.

---

*Morbidity and Mortality Weekly Report (U.S. Centers for Disease Control, U.S. Public Health Service, Atlanta, Georgia) carries regular progress notes on the frequency and success of treatment of genital herpes. Check index issues to find individual reports between 1985 and current date. This is an ongoing surveillance.

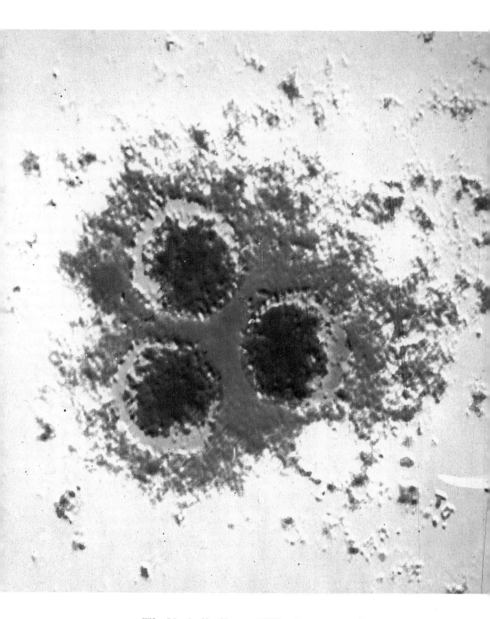

*The Varicella-Zoster (VZ) virus, a member
of the herpes virus group. This virus
causes chicken pox and shingles.*

POLIO AND OTHER KILLERS

One of the deadliest of all viral infections, paralytic poliomyelitis, used to strike down thousands of young people in the United States each year, killing many and permanently crippling many more. Although the polio virus is basically an intestinal virus, it can sometimes migrate to the spinal cord and destroy nerve cells there that control muscular movement all over the body. Partial or complete paralysis can result, and once the nerve cells are dead the muscles can never recover their function. When the virus attacks cells very high in the spinal cord, the result is an extremely dangerous condition known as *bulbar polio*. Nerve cells located there control the muscles necessary for swallowing and even breathing. When these are destroyed, the disease has an extremely high death rate.

Thanks to the widespread use of vaccines, polio in the United States is now exceedingly uncommon, but the threat of polio is by no means eliminated. All babies and children should have full, up-to-date immunization, and any adult under the age of forty should make sure his or her polio immunization was completed. More than anyone else, it is young adults who are hardest hit when polio strikes.

A few other viral diseases, once deadly killers, have also been controlled, thanks to worldwide vaccination programs and public health measures. Yellow fever, once a widespread epidemic disease, is now seldom seen in humans, although the virus still causes sporadic epidemics among tropical monkeys. As for smallpox, the last reported case in the entire world occurred over fifteen years ago. World health officials now believe the disease may at last have been permanently stamped out—the first infectious killer in all history to have been eradicated thanks to a deliberate effort by humans.

Still other viral diseases are particularly notable be-

*Dr. Albert Sabin, discoverer of the oral polio
vaccine, examines a patient in a polio ward in 1967.
Thanks to polio vaccines, polio is now rare.*

cause of certain unique characteristics. In mumps, once common in children, the virus attacks cells in the salivary glands, causing a painful swelling of the cheeks and under the chin. Mumps is relatively harmless to small children, but in teenagers or young adults the virus may also attack cells in the testicles of the male or the ovaries of the female and—especially in the male—may cause permanent sterility, the inability to have children. Because of this threat, children are now routinely vaccinated with a long-acting vaccine, and mumps has become uncommon in this country.

Because the *rubeola virus* that causes red measles can sometimes cause a dangerous *encephalitis* (brain fever) or pneumonia or other complications, a measles vaccine was considered a great breakthrough when it was developed in the 1960s. By vaccinating all children in infancy, health officials hoped that measles, like smallpox, would be completely eradicated within a few years. Sad to say, that has not happened. The early measles vaccine was not completely effective and didn't protect against the disease for as long as doctors had predicted. As a result, whole new epidemics of measles began appearing again in the late 1980s, particularly among teenagers and young adults. Today young children are given booster shots with newer, more effective vaccines, and teenagers are urged to have fresh boosters to extend their protection. Vaccination against *rubella*, or German measles, is also recommended, especially for girls before they reach childbearing age. German measles doesn't cause any great problem for the children or young adults who contract it, but it can cause serious malformations in developing unborn babies if a mother-to-be gets the disease during the first half of her pregnancy.

Modern scientists are still discovering new and unexpected kinds of viral diseases. In 1957, for example, American virologist Carleton Gajdusek began studying a strange form of brain deterioration known as *kuru*—"the shivering disease"—long known to afflict members of certain native tribes in New Guinea. After eight years of work, Gajdusek finally isolated the cause, one of the tiniest viruses ever discovered. This strange virus would live in a victim's body for years, successfully hiding from natural immune defenses and slowly destroying brain cells, one by one, all the while. It was one of the first *retroviruses* (RNA-only viruses) ever identified, and its ill effects showed up only after many years of infection. It attacked New Guinea natives for a bizarre reason: a form of ritual cannibalism was a part of their culture, and they became infected by eating the infected brains of victims.

THE WORST ONE OF THEM ALL

Although many virus diseases have been around for centuries, not all of them are that old. In fact, the worst virus plague ever encountered made its first recognized appearance in the early 1980s and is still spreading in a growing epidemic today. This, of course, is the infection caused by the *human immunodeficiency virus*, or HIV, which can lead to the deadly disease called the *acquired immune deficiency syndrome*, or AIDS.

You'll remember that we talked about retroviruses and how they work back in Chapter 3. These are comparatively uncommon RNA-only viruses that require a special helper enzyme called reverse transcriptase in order to multiply inside a host cell. HIV—the AIDS virus—is just such a retrovirus, or RNA virus, which contains its own reverse transcriptase enzyme. This enables it to "write its single-strand RNA code backward" into DNA so that new virus particles can be made inside the infected host cells. Nobody knows for sure where this dangerous virus came from. Scientists now believe that a few isolated cases of AIDS began appearing, completely unrecognized, as early as the 1950s. But it was not until 1980 that a clear-cut disease pattern began to appear in ever-increasing numbers of people in Africa, Europe, and the United States. The causative HIV virus was identified in 1982 by French virologist Dr. Luc Montagnier and American virologist Dr. Robert Gallo and their laboratory teams. Unfortunately, that HIV virus has proved to be one of the most dangerous viruses ever encountered in all history.

Why is it so dangerous? As we've seen, each disease-causing virus has a favorite kind of host cell that it seeks out when it invades the body. Unlike other viruses, HIV—the AIDS virus—seeks out certain special kinds of white blood cells as its favorite host cells. These cells are known as *macrophages* and *T4 lymphocytes*. Once inside host macrophages, the virus particles seem just to take up lodging and travel with those cells to distant parts of the body, including brain cells, which HIV can also then infect. But once inside the T4 lymphocytes, the virus forces those cells to replicate more and more HIV virus particles. Then they burst out into the bloodstream and other body fluids, including the man's semen and the woman's vaginal fluids, leaving the dead T4 cells behind them.

The reason the AIDS virus is so extremely dangerous is that the white cells they infect—the macrophages and the T4 lymphocytes—are the very backbone of the body's *immune protective system*, the one organ system we depend upon the most to guard and protect us against virus infections. Without a strong immune protective system, we die—it's as simple as that. And as more and more T4 cells are destroyed, the victim's immune system grows weaker and weaker. It can no longer fight off many different infections that can get going in the body only when the immune system is weak. It can no longer fight off certain cancers that are normally held in check by the healthy immune system. As an end result of HIV infection, the victim begins to develop the signs and symptoms of AIDS with its accompanying so-called *opportunistic infections*—

infections that seize the opportunity to strike when the immune system is weakened or destroyed, and the victim ultimately dies of AIDS.

For more detail about the behavior of HIV or the development of AIDS, a number of excellent books are available.* The important point here is that new and dangerous virus infections continue to appear, apparently out of the blue, to this very day. And if there is any silver lining at all to the AIDS epidemic, it is that the appearance of this disease, more than anything else, has vastly stimulated basic research into the nature of viruses and their diseases in general—research that equips us not only to fight new virus threats but to better deal with old ones as well.

TREATING VIRUS INFECTIONS

What can be done to treat virus infections once they occur? For many years there was virtually no effective form of active treatment. Viruses are not affected by the antibiotics that stop bacterial infections so swiftly. For the vast majority of viral infections, the best known treatment even today is adequate rest, a nourishing diet, and patience enough to wait for the body's own natural defenses to come to the rescue. While waiting, simple medicines can sometimes alleviate the more uncomfortable symptoms: acetaminophen (Tylenol or Datril) for headaches and aching muscles; nose drops and cough syrups for upper respiratory symptoms; and antinausea and antidiarrhea medicines for gastrointestinal symptoms.

---

*The current "bible" on HIV infection and AIDS is DeVita et al., editors, AIDS (New York: Lippincott/Harper Collins, 1989). This is a medical textbook. For more understandable books about HIV infection and AIDS, see Alan E. Nourse, M.D., AIDS, revised edition (New York: Franklin Watts, 1989), or check with your librarian for many other up-to-date titles.

In recent years, a few antiviral drugs have been discovered which *do* help slow down or prevent certain viral infections. A drug called *amantadine*, for example, seems to block infections caused by type A influenza viruses. Another drug known as *acyclovir* (ace-EYE-clo-vir) used in ointment or pill form can markedly reduce the frequency and severity of recurrent genital herpes attacks, although it doesn't cure the infection. At least one drug, *zidovudine*, or AZT, has been shown to slow down the reproduction of HIV in an infected person, relieving symptoms in people with symptomatic AIDS and possibly postponing the development of symptoms if given early enough. And, in addition, a whole new variety of other possible antiviral drugs is being investigated and tested today because of the AIDS epidemic. We'll talk in more detail about how some of these drugs work and about what lies in the future with antiviral drugs in Chapter 5 and Chapter 6.

Today, however, we must still rely on the body's own built-in capacity to resist and fight off viral invaders— the body's natural protective immune system—and on vaccines that can stimulate the immune system to actually prevent many virus infections. Obviously, with treatment so difficult, it is far better to prevent virus diseases in the first place, when possible, with the use of effective vaccines. The story of how those vaccines were first developed and how they work to prevent viral infection makes one of the most exciting chapters in the history of medical discovery, a chapter that is still opening up today.

SOME VIRUS BAD ACTORS YOU SHOULD KNOW ABOUT

Virus	Disease It Causes	Organ System Attacked	Symptoms	Usual Outcome	Vaccine?
Rhinoviruses & Adenoviruses	Head colds	Nasal mucosa, throat, bronchi	Coughing, sneezing, runny nose	Clears up spontaneously after a few days	Yes, but very ineffective
Influenza viruses	Influenza or "flu"	Whole body, especially upper respiratory track, muscles	Fever, aching muscles, fatigue, cough	Secondary pneumonia can complicate or kill	Yes, but new vaccine used each year
HIV (human immunodeficiency virus)	AIDS	Immune system, brain, skin, other organs	Opportunistic infections, dementia, skin cancers	Ultimately fatal	No vaccine as yet
Rubeola	Red measles; sometimes measles encephalitis (brain fever)	Whole body	Red skin rash, fever, sore throat, cough	Usually clears up in two weeks, but measles encephalitis may complicate	Yes; widely used and recommended
Rubella	German measles	Whole body; especially attacks unborn baby	Brief red skin rash, fever	Clears up in 3–4 days, but may deform unborn baby	Yes, especially for young mothers-to-be
Mumps	Mumps (infection of salivary glands, sometimes testicles and ovaries)	Salivary glands primarily; sometimes testicles or ovaries in older children	Painful, swollen glands in cheeks, under chin	Clears up in 2–3 weeks	Yes, given as part of "baby shots"
HSV (Herpes simplex virus 1 & 2)	HSV 1 causes cold sores. HSV 2 causes genital herpes. Sometimes interchangeable.	HSV 1: cold sores on lips, nose, around mouth. HSV 2: both male and female genitals.	Sores around lips (HSV 1) or painful sores on genitals (HSV 2)	Clears up spontaneously, but HSV 2 may recur again and again	No
Herpes zoster virus	Chicken pox. Later may recur as shingles.	Whole body. Causes itchy vesicular rash all over body in children or previously uninfected adults.	Itchy rash like little water blisters. Fever, cough.	Clears up in 6–10 days; no scarring from blisters. Shingles cause painful skin rash.	Nearly perfected but not used in U.S. yet
EBV (Epstein-Barr virus)	Infectious mononucleosis	Whole body, especially lymph glands, spleen, skin. Related to certain rare cancers.	Swollen glands, abdominal pain, fever, skin rash	Takes weeks for recovery	No

Disease	Cause	Description	Symptoms	Outcome	Vaccine
Smallpox	Smallpox	Whole body, especially a permanently pitting rash of skin; attacks brain and respiratory system. Eradicated since 1974.	Fever, scarring skin rash	Used to take weeks for recovery, high mortality rate. Now eradicated by worldwide vaccination.	Yes, but no longer necessary
Yellow fever	Yellow fever virus	Attacks and destroys liver cells. Spread by bite of infected anopheles mosquitos. Largely confined to tropics.	Abdominal pain, liver swelling, jaundice (yellow skin color)	Frequently fatal	Yes, very effective and long-lasting
Rabies	Rabies in animals and humans	Endemic throughout the world. Spread by bite of infected wild or domestic animals (dogs, cats, skunks, raccoons, bats, etc.).	Fever, paralysis, throat spasm on swallowing	Fatal unless vaccine is used in time	Yes
Poliomyelitis	Polio viruses	Intestinal tract primarily, but often spreads to cells in spinal cord and/or brainstem causing permanent paralysis.	Intestinal symptoms unnoticeable. In severe cases, paralysis of legs, arms, respiratory muscles. Fever.	Fatal in severe cases. Permanent paralysis when paralysis occurs.	Yes; both Salk (injection) or Sabin (oral) but Sabin preferred
Hepatitis A	Hepatitis A	Attacks liver cells. Spread by contaminated stool or other intestinal fluids.	Liver swelling and pain. Jaundice (yellow coloring) to skin, whites of eyes. Fever.	Sometimes fatal; long recovery.	No. Gamma globulin may prevent infection after exposure.
Hepatitis B	Hepatitis B	Attacks & destroys liver cells. Spread by sexual contact, sharing of dirty injection needles. Many recovered victims remain lifelong carriers spreading the virus.	Fever, jaundice, liver pain, exhaustion	Fatal for 10%. 30% of recoverees remain virus carriers.	Yes. Especially recommended for health care workers, those known exposed.
Hepatitis C (formerly known as hepatitis non-A, non-B)	Hepatitis C	Like hepatitis B, attacks liver cells. A milder attack, but victims remain lifelong carriers and spreaders of the virus.	Fever, abdominal pain. Less severe illness.	Most recover, but many remain lifelong carriers of the virus.	No

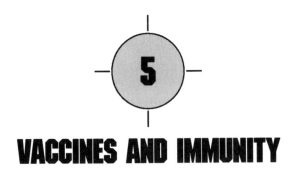

VACCINES AND IMMUNITY

From the very beginning of virus research, medical scientists faced a perplexing question. Obviously viruses could produce many severe, even fatal, infections in humans. Just as obviously, we seemed to have no effective ways to cure viral infections after they had started. Why, then, hadn't everybody died of virus infections centuries ago?

The fact is that we do have some very effective defenses against viral infections—not external defenses involving miracle drugs and medical treatments, but natural *internal* defenses. There isn't much outward evidence that these defenses even exist, but if a person manages to survive the initial virus invasion long enough, his or her body alone will sooner or later fight off most viral infections. Swift, deadly viruses such as rabies, yellow fever, and smallpox killed most victims quickly, before their natural defenses could be rallied. But for those who did survive, internal protection against future infections by the same virus seemed to linger on long after the virus was conquered, rendering the victim *immune* (from a Latin word meaning "exempt") from recurrent infection.

What is the nature of this immune defense system? How does it work? Can weak defenses be strengthened or speeded up? Can immunity be artificially stimulated against all kinds of virus infections, just as it was against smallpox and rabies back in the days before viruses were even discovered? These are questions virologists have been asking since the earliest days of virus research. In recent years some very encouraging answers have appeared.

ANTIGENS AND ANTIBODIES

Our natural defenses against viruses depend upon a complex and remarkable system of cells and chemicals known as *the immune system*. When a virus invades the body, the very presence of the invader triggers this immune system into a vast, body-wide chain reaction designed to destroy or immobilize the invader as quickly as possible.*

As far as the immune system is concerned, every substance and cell within the body falls into one of two categories: *self* or *not-self*. Anything that naturally belongs in the body is considered self and is okay. Anything foreign to the body—any cell or protein from outside the body, for instance, that happens to get inside—is considered not-self and therefore not okay, or dangerous. This dividing line between self and not-self is individual and unique to *your* body and *yours alone*—any cells or proteins from almost anybody else's body that might get into yours, even from your own brother or sister, would be considered not-self by your immune system, unless your brother or sister is your identical twin, developed from the same original fertilized egg cell—and even then the match might not be absolutely perfect.

In simple terms, this means that whenever a strange, foreign, or not-self substance gets into your body, especially a foreign protein, your immune system senses that

*For details about how the immune system does this, see Alan E. Nourse, M.D., *Your Immune System*, revised edition (New York: Franklin Watts, 1989). See also For Further Reading on page 93 of this book, *The Virus Invaders*.

it does not belong there and begins a complex internal chain reaction of events to get rid of it, or to at least block it from further contact with your body's cells and tissues. Mere *external* contact with such a substance doesn't normally set this machinery in motion. We are constantly touching foreign substances, even eating a wide variety of foreign proteins, carbohydrates, and other substances for nourishment, without harmful effects. But let even a tiny bit of foreign protein material—a pollen grain, for instance, or a protein-coated virus particle—get into the tissues under the skin, or work its way through the mucous membrane of the lungs or the intestine into the interior of the body, and the alarm goes off and a widespread reaction begins.

First, special patrolling white blood cells called T-lymphocytes and macrophages, wandering throughout all the tissues of the body, come in contact with the invading foreign protein (or *antigen*, to use the technical term). On their surfaces these white blood cells carry *receptor* protein molecules that actually touch the foreign protein and recognize it as foreign, or not-self and, in effect, take its measurements. The T-lymphocytes then carry the message and the measurements back to other white cells, which respond by manufacturing special protein entities known as *antibodies* and dumping them into the bloodstream. These antibodies then flock to the place where the foreign protein has entered and work to destroy or neutralize it.

We know that each antibody is made to measure, or "form-fitted," to its particular antigen so perfectly that it is capable of immobilizing that specific antigen and no other. An antibody is shaped to fit around its corresponding antigen the way a lock fits around a key. Modern researchers, using an amazing technique known as *X-ray crystallography*, have actually shown that the three-dimensional structure of a given antibody's protein molecules has bumps and grooves that perfectly fit into corresponding bumps and grooves on the appropriate antigen's protein molecules. We also know that the invading viruses have surface protein molecules that must attach themselves to matching receptor protein molecules on the surface of susceptible cells in order to invade those cells. One way that the antibodies can block these invading virus particles is to clamp onto the virus's surface protein molecules and prevent them from attaching themselves to the cell's receptor molecules in the first place. The virus particles are then, in effect, held as helpless prisoners until white blood cells known as *phagocytes* can engulf and destroy them. The sheer beauty and simplicity of this system is simply mind-boggling. How could it ever have come about? So far, nobody knows for sure, but it *happens*!

Unfortunately, this antigen-antibody reaction takes time to get started after a viral invasion. This means that viral infections can often become well entrenched before sufficient opposing antibodies can be manufactured. And the antibodies can do nothing about the viruses that have already invaded the victim's cells. All they can do is help immobilize and destroy the new virus particles being produced and released from the already infected cells. Other elements of the immune system can attack the infected cells themselves, but they require time to be mobilized and dispatched, too.

If the initial wave of infection is not too severe, enough antibodies will eventually form to neutralize all the new virus particles being formed, and the victim will gradually recover from the infection. What is more, in many cases these antibodies continue to be manufactured, or remain present in the body for months or even years after the viral infection is over. This protects the victim if that particular virus attempts another invasion. Certain elements of the immune system even seem to retain a "memory" of the shape of the viral antigens so that whenever those particular antigens reappear, new antibodies against them can be formed much more quickly and effectively. Thus, as a result of the first infection, the victim may remain immune to reinfection from the same virus source for years, sometimes even a lifetime.

Some viruses, however, are an exception. Viruses of the herpesvirus family, for example, and hepatitis B viruses have found ways to evade complete destruction by the immune system, and they can remain in the body, inactive but present, for long periods of time, even when the acute infection is controlled and stopped. Thus a person once infected by the genital herpes virus may have recurrent attacks later on, and many recovered hepatitis B victims remain *carriers* of the virus in their bloodstreams for years, perfectly able to pass the virus to others.

THE SEARCH FOR VACCINES

Doctors speak of the immunity that arises from an actual previous infection as *active immunity*. Because it can last for a very long time, this is the best possible protection against reinfection by the same virus. Smallpox victims, for example, only got smallpox once. If they survived the first attack, they never got smallpox again, no matter how much contact they had with the virus.

Fortunately, there are several ways to *stimulate* protective immunity to a virus without risking the infection itself. For instance, one person's immunity can sometimes be passed on to others simply by passing some of the immune person's antibodies to a susceptible person. This is what protects infant babies from certain viral infections during the first few months of their lives. If an expectant mother has had measles sometime earlier in her life or has been effectively immunized with measles shots, some of the mother's antibodies against the measles virus will cross into the baby's bloodstream while she is carrying the fetus, so that the newborn baby will be immune to measles for some months after birth.

Doctors speak of this as *passive immunity*, or passively acquired immunity. It can work in other ways, too. If a person who has never had mumps or mumps shots, for example, is exposed to the disease, he or she can receive an inoculation of blood serum from someone who has recently recovered from a mumps infection, and will develop an acquired immunity for a long enough period to keep from being infected by the exposure. The main trouble with such acquired immunity is that it doesn't last very long. The acquired antibodies will soon disappear from the recipient's bloodstream, leaving him or her vulnerable again within a few weeks or months.

This doesn't mean that acquired immunity is useless. It *does* protect newborn babies from diseases such as measles and whooping cough until their bodies and immune systems have grown strong enough to see them through— or preferably until they can be actively immunized against such diseases with their early baby shots. And if an unprotected person is exposed to a dangerous viral infection like hepatitis A, even a brief immunity acquired from gamma globulin injections can be a lifesaver. (Gamma globulin is the portion of an immune donor's blood serum that contains antibodies.) But for many of the viral diseases, a long-lasting active immunity would be far preferable.

One way to achieve this was suggested by Edward Jenner's famous smallpox vaccination experiment. Jenner didn't know why his patients became immune to the dreaded smallpox just by being subjected to a mild case of cowpox; it was enough that it worked. Today we know why. Although the live vaccinia virus of cowpox causes only a mild localized infection compared to the ravages of the smallpox virus, the two viruses happened to carry antigens that were so very similar that the body's antibody factories couldn't tell them apart. The antibodies formed in response to the mild cowpox virus blocked the more virulent smallpox virus as well.

This basic principle, once it was understood, was very important. Introducing a living virus into the human body, in one form or another, could trigger the immune system to produce protective antibodies, leading to lasting active immunity. If somehow this could be done without risking dangerous illness from the invading virus, successful vaccines might be made against almost any virus infection.

But how? As we saw earlier, researchers had demonstrated that it was the nucleic acid packet at the core of the virus that was the infective part, and yet *proteins* were the most potent antigens. Perhaps it was the protein coating of the virus that triggered the formation of antibodies. If this was so, then destroying the virus's infective core before it was used for injection as a vaccine might strip it of its power to cause infection, yet still preserve the antibody-stimulating protein. The person inoculated with such a vaccine should be safe from infection and at the same time might develop a long-lasting active immunity to the virus.

It seemed like a long shot, but it worked. The most familiar example of a successful *killed virus vaccine* was the one developed by Dr. Jonas Salk and his team at the University of Pittsburgh in 1953 against the three major strains of polio viruses. Salk killed the virulent viruses with formaldehyde before injecting them as a vaccine. Just as he hoped, their protein shells alone triggered the formation of anti-polio antibodies. Those who were vaccinated with this killed virus vaccine developed active immunity to polio for the first time, and a dramatic mass vaccination program conducted in 1955 brought to an end the dreadful annual polio epidemics in the United States in a matter of two or three short years.

Unfortunately there were problems with the Salk vaccine. Four separate shots were required to build a lasting immunity. Perhaps more serious, antibodies formed against the injected vaccine did not adequately block the reproduction of polio viruses in the intestinal tract—which was, after all, their natural habitat—so that the spread of the wild virus was not completely controlled.

Thus a different approach to creating a polio vaccine was considered. Rather than killing the polio viruses, Dr. Albert Sabin of the University of Cincinnati College of Medicine tried attenuating, or weakening, them severely by passing them repeatedly through animal or egg cultures. Nobody was entirely sure *why* this process weakened the viruses, but after many such passages the viruses, although still very much alive, were found to be weakened to the point that they could not cause dangerous disease.* In contrast to the wild polio viruses in nature, these were "tame" viruses. In 1955, Sabin began testing a polio vaccine made of such live but attenuated viruses. That vaccine was found both safe and effective and was approved for general use in the United States in 1961.

The Sabin polio vaccine had two distinct advantages. It could be taken by mouth instead of by injection, and it produced immunity to polio viruses in the intestine as well as in the bloodstream. Universal use of the Salk and Sabin vaccines in the United States had an immediate and dramatic effect. Within a very few years the incidence of paralytic polio in this country dropped from 35,000 cases a year to practically zero—only three or four cases reported each year! And that record is still maintained today.

THE MEASLES VACCINE

Yet another means was used to guard against the possible side effects of a vaccine made from live, attenuated viruses when the earliest vaccine against rubeola (red measles)

---

*This was, of course, very similar to the process that Louis Pasteur used to weaken rabies viruses in order to make his rabies vaccine, as we saw in Chapter 1. He didn't know why it worked, either, but it did.

was developed. Because measles complications such as encephalitis (brain fever) and pneumonia could cripple or kill people, widespread measles shots were recommended as soon as a measles vaccine had been developed, in the hope of wiping out measles, just as polio had been wiped out. Unfortunately, however, when the first measles vaccine was made from live but inactivated rubeola viruses, the vaccine itself caused mild cases of measles, with complications appearing in rare cases. To prevent this, an injection of gamma globulin was given along with the measles vaccine. This successfully suppressed any measles symptoms arising from the vaccine itself until the body had enough time to build its own long-lasting anti-rubeola antibodies.

As it turned out, measles was *not* wiped out by widespread measles vaccination, because early vaccines were not as effective or as long-lasting as people had hoped. Today public health authorities recommend that young children have a measles vaccine booster after the initial vaccination, using improved and updated vaccines, and that adolescents and young adults have measles boosters even though they were previously vaccinated in childhood. Unfortunately, we still have a long way to go to wipe out measles.

A CONTINUING SEARCH

The development of new vaccines continued and still continues even today. In the late 1970s, for example, scientists at the University of California at San Francisco finally perfected a vaccine against hepatitis B, even though no way could be found to grow the virus itself in the laboratory. The vaccine was made not from the virus proper but from a special surface protein surrounding the virus core, which could act as an antibody-stimulating antigen. By using newly developed techniques of *genetic engineering*, the California researchers found a way to cause a simple strain of intestinal bacteria to produce large quantities of the necessary surface protein safely and inexpensively in the laboratory. As we saw earlier, the hepatitis B vaccine was approved by the FDA in 1981 and is now available to protect people at high risk of contracting hepatitis B.

Other vaccine research has not worked out so well. Malaria, a disease caused by a protozoan blood parasite that is passed to humans through the bites of infected mosquitoes, kills some five *million* people worldwide every year. An effective malaria vaccine would be a godsend—but so far no such vaccine has emerged. For one thing, there are several different strains of malarial parasite, each antigenically different from the others. For another, the infecting parasite goes through several distinct stages of development inside the body, each stage antigenically different from the others. For several years now there have been reports from various laboratories that a truly effective malaria vaccine is almost ready, but so far none has yet proved successful.

Of course today, with the AIDS epidemic in full swing, an enormous amount of research has been devoted to finding an effective vaccine against HIV. That also would be a godsend, and this work may well bear fruit—sooner or later. In all history there has never been a virus more thoroughly studied, nor a more intense search for some protein element of HIV that might be used as an antibody-stimulating antigen in a vaccine. And indeed, several "candidate vaccines" have been developed in various AIDS laboratories. But here researchers face a terrible dilemma: how to test such candidate vaccines to be sure beyond doubt that they are 100 percent safe to use. AIDS is far too dreadful a disease to take any possible chance that the disease might be transmitted by a vaccine. There are grave ethical questions involved in testing such vaccines on uninfected humans. But the only other species that can be infected by HIV is the chimpanzee—and

A highly magnified photograph of the mosquito that carries malaria, shown perched on a human finger

Lab technicians check the baboons they use in their medical research. Animals like these baboons are in very short supply for medical research.

chimpanzees for such research are in impossibly short supply. There simply aren't enough of them available for fast, effective testing of a vaccine. To compound the problem, animal rights activists are working fiercely day and night to prevent chimpanzees from being used in this manner. In the meantime, hundreds of human beings who could be protected by a vaccine are becoming HIV-infected every day as the epidemic spreads, and vaccine research is bogged down in delays, withheld funding, ethical debates, and red tape.

Important as vaccine research may be, it is by no means the only direction that modern virus research is leading us. New and exciting work is being done today to study the basic biochemical nature of viruses, the many effects they can have on living creatures, and the long-term roles they may play in such areas as the development of cancer, the phenomenon of aging, and indeed the alterations they may make in the basic genetic nature of our cells. The story of the virus invaders would not be complete without a chapter, still being written today, on some of the new directions virus research is taking.

MODERN VIRUS RESEARCH

From the very beginning, virus researchers have worked toward two major and overriding goals: to find out what viruses are and how they behave; and to find ways to cure, control, or prevent dangerous viral diseases.

Where does this research stand today? Although specific cures for viral diseases have yet to be found, many of the most deadly viral diseases can now be prevented and epidemics can be controlled by vaccination. In addition to smallpox, yellow fever, and poliomyelitis, the list of preventable viral diseases now includes rubeola, rubella, mumps, hepatitis B, and many strains of influenza. Of course today prevention of infection by HIV, the AIDS virus, is an urgent challenge of highest priority, and prevention of certain other viral infections such as *equine encephalitis*, a brain-destroying virus disease, are high on the list of challenges. In addition to vaccines, scientists are also searching for drugs or other agents to stop, or at least to modify, many other viral diseases. Among the most interesting of these other agents is a naturally occurring substance known as *human interferon*.

A NATURAL VIRUS KILLER

In 1957 a Scottish virologist, Alick Isaacs, and a Swiss microbiologist, Jean Lindenman, discovered a natural protein substance in the bloodstream that seemed to interfere with the reproduction of viruses in infected cells and thus block the development of viral infection. The substance, called *interferon*, was produced by white blood cells in people whose bodies had been stimulated by a viral invasion. Later other forms of interferon were discovered. And the body also produces somewhat similar defensive proteins known as *interleukins*. All of these substances are in a general class known as *lymphokines*.

At first it was hoped that the interferons might be used as medicines to combat a wide variety of viral infections quite dramatically. When the tiny amounts available were tested against cold viruses, for instance, they seemed quite effective in preventing colds. But these substances produced very toxic side effects when used as medicines, and they could be extracted from human blood only in tiny amounts, which made them far too expensive for practical use.

Then in the late 1970s it was found that interferons seemed to slow the growth of certain kinds of cancers in laboratory animals. This fit in with the growing suspicion that certain viruses might help trigger the wild, uncontrolled growth that occurs in cancer cells. In 1978 the American Cancer Society sponsored a large study to evaluate the use of interferons to treat cancers in humans. The American Cancer Society study was possible because by then researchers could produce large quantities of interferons quite cheaply from laboratory yeast cell cultures, using genetic engineering techniques. We still don't know just how useful—or practical—these substances may prove to be in fighting cancer, but such studies have brought the whole question of a virus-cancer connection into very sharp focus.

VIRUSES AND CANCER

Once scientists discovered that viruses were really just tiny, encapsulated bits of hereditary material capable of causing permanent and inheritable changes in the cells of their hosts, they realized that they had within their grasp a way to study the hereditary patterns of normal and abnormal cells alike—perhaps even including cancer cells.

The idea that viruses might be involved in some way with the development of cancer has been around for almost as long as viruses themselves have been known. As early as 1908, Danish researchers Wilhelm Ellerman and Olaf Bang had shown that certain animal viruses could cause a form of *leukemia* (a cancer of the blood) in chickens, although nobody knew how or why. In 1911 an American physician, Francis Peyton Rous, developed a clear filtrate from certain tumors in chickens that could, by itself, produce new tumors in healthy chickens. For a while there was a flurry of activity to try to identify viruses with cancers in higher animals and humans. But by the time some really suggestive evidence of a true virus-cancer link began to appear in the early 1930s, nobody was much interested anymore.

Why not? For one thing, the evidence was very vague, and the link, if any, between viruses and cancer didn't seem to be direct. If it was part of the picture, it was only a small part. More important, a number of other factors far removed from viruses had been implicated more directly in various human cancers. Excessive exposure to X rays and other kinds of radiation, for example, was clearly linked to cancer formation. So was exposure to certain so-called *carcinogenic*, or cancer-causing, chemicals. On the other hand, there was not even a single instance of any virus that had been cultured and identified from human cancer tissue. Unfortunately, those early workers didn't yet know enough about viruses to realize that a virus-induced change within a cell might be passed on from generation to generation within the host cell, perhaps leading to cancerous changes sometime later. This could happen even after the virus that had caused the change in the first place was no longer present—at least not in the form of a recognizable virus. But as new knowledge about the nature and behavior of viruses piled up, more and more researchers began to reconsider the whole question.

As we have seen, every virus is made up of two parts: an outer shell composed of protein and an inner core made up of nucleic acid in the form of either DNA or RNA. What is more, viral DNA and RNA are very similar to the DNA and RNA found in the nuclei of all living cells. In the cell nucleus this hereditary material is concentrated in thousands of little packets known as genes, strung together like beads on a thread, to form chromosomes.

THE MASTER MOLECULES

It is the DNA in the genes, and their particular location on a chromosome, that determines the characteristics of the daughter cells when the parent cells reproduce by cell division. If, for some reason, a gene or a group of genes breaks off from its chromosome or becomes displaced from its normal location before cell division occurs, the daughter cells may be markedly different from the parent cell. These differences will be passed on to the next generation of cells, and the next, and the next, and so on.

But the genes in living cells control far more than just the heredity of those cells. The DNA and RNA in genes act as master molecules, controlling virtually every aspect of the cell's structure and behavior. Some genes control the manufacture of proteins and enzymes within the cell. Others monitor the energy-producing reactions that occur within the cell. And, very significantly, still others control how fast or how slowly the cell will grow and reproduce and in what kind of tissue the cell can grow.

How can genes do this? They can't think. They don't "know" what they're supposed to be doing, any more than a light switch on the wall "knows" that it is supposed to turn the current on or off at any given time. In fact, a gene is very much like an on-or-off light switch. Its master molecules may either switch a chemical process *on* when it's supposed to, or switch it *off* when it's supposed to. (By "supposed to" we simply mean the way it is *programmed* to by the molecular arrangement of the gene.) The master molecules in another gene may *prevent* that same chemical process from being switched on or off when it's supposed to. And when a gene malfunctions, much as a defective light switch might, it may *fail* to switch a chemical process on or off when it's supposed to, or fail to *prevent* it from being switched on or off when it's supposed to.

Now imagine that the chemical process we're talking about is a signal to the cell to "grow and divide in a slow, orderly manner in the right kind of tissue only." If a defective signal is given, the message may be changed to "grow and divide like mad in *any* kind of tissue, and *don't stop*," or, in effect, "become a cancer cell." This is exactly how important gene control, or the lack of it, can be in just one vital area, the control of cell growth in the body.

Ordinarily, cell reproduction is very orderly. Except during periods of accelerated body growth or sudden maturation—during infancy or adolescence, for example—new cells are normally produced only when needed to replace old, worn-out cells. What is more, cells making up one kind of tissue will ordinarily grow only in that kind of tissue and no other. Bone cells grow in bone, muscle cells in muscle, and so forth. But if something happens to alter the orderly gene control of cell growth, certain cells may begin to reproduce rapidly and wildly, regardless of need and totally out of control. Even worse, the special characteristics that distinguish a cell of bone tissue, muscle tissue, or glandular tissue may be lost, so that a cell that originally would grow only in its own kind of tissue begins to invade surrounding tissues. Control of cell growth may be so completely disrupted that these sick, abnormal cells break loose from their neighbors and travel through the bloodstream or lymph channels to lodge in distant places and develop new clusters of sick, wildly growing cells. It is precisely this type of wild and invasive cell growth that we know as *cancer*.

With this in mind, we can see why scientists today are quite certain that some kind of connection exists between viruses and cancer—at least some forms of cancer. We've seen that the DNA or RNA in a virus can take over a host cell's chemical factories and force the cell to manufacture nothing but viral DNA or RNA and viral proteins. In a matter of minutes after virus invasion, that cell may be totally exhausted by building new virus particles. It finally bursts apart, scattering hundreds of new viruses abroad to infect more cells. But certain viruses behave differently. They may simply attach their DNA or RNA to that already present in the cell nucleus and then sit and wait. No new viruses are formed. In fact, all apparent traces of the invading virus may vanish except for that fragment of viral DNA or RNA tacked onto the cell's hereditary material. But when that cell reproduces itself, it reproduces the viral DNA fragment right along with its own. In effect, the virus has silently altered the host cell's hereditary mechanism. Some new messages have been added to the cell's genetic code, and these new messages are passed on from one generation of the cell to the next.

In many cases the end result of this is simply that the cell proceeds merrily on its way until something triggers the viral DNA or RNA to take over the cell's life functions and start producing more virus particles. But those virus genes might have an even more profound effect on the cell. They might, for instance, override or confuse the cell's normal "grow and divide slowly" signal and substitute a "grow and divide rapidly and don't stop" signal, transforming the cell into a cancer cell that then begins dividing wildly, out of control.

Scientists today believe that this is at least one of the ways in which cancers can arise in lower animals and human beings. The virus connection is sneaky because it isn't direct. It may simply alter one signal, which alters the effect of another signal, which alters the effect of still another signal. Or possibly two or three other injuries or alterations completely independent of the virus effect must occur to the cell before the changed virus signal makes any difference. There doesn't need to be an identifiable living virus present in the cancer tissue for all this to happen. Only a fragment of altered hereditary material in the pre-cancerous cells would be needed. Nor would such a change from normal cell growth to cancerous growth necessarily have to begin immediately or all at once. The altered cells might well remain quiet for years, maybe even decades, until some outside influence came along—exposure to excessive radiation, for example, or years of continuous exposure to carcinogenic chemicals such as the tars in tobacco smoke—to trigger the outburst of wild growth. It may be, in fact, that a whole succession, or cascade, of events must occur for a cancer to develop, with the virus playing just one small but essentially deadly part in the whole series of events.

Whatever the details may prove to be, virus researchers are hard at work studying how such a virus-cancer connection might operate in humans. Consider, for example, the *human papilloma viruses* that cause genital warts, an increasingly common sexually transmitted infection. These viruses invade cells in the woman's *cervix*, or mouth of the womb. We now know that papilloma virus infections are associated with the early and sudden appearance of cancer of the cervix. As the frequency of genital wart infections increases among teenage girls, more and more of these girls are turning up with cancer of the cervix in their teens or young adult years. This is a marked change in the pattern of this cancer that has just appeared in recent years. This may sound like bad news in the short run, but as the connection between viruses and cancer is more clearly understood, it could be a happy day for the future of human health in the long run. As American physician and virologist Dr. Robert Huebner recently put it, "If viruses are a key to certain cancers, we can handle it. We can find ways to control, perhaps prevent, those cancers."

OTHER DIRECTIONS, OTHER GOALS

Meanwhile, virus researchers are learning more about the basic nature and behavior of viruses in general. In 1965 Dr. S. Speigelman produced in his laboratory a synthetic (artificial) RNA molecule that had the power to infect living cells. In effect, he had produced an artificial virus! Two years later, in 1967, Drs. A. Kornberg, N. Goulian, and R. L. Sinsheimer went a step further and put together synthetic viral DNA. This substance could not only infect living cells but could also take control of the cells' biochemical functions, just as natural viruses do. When the infected cells burst apart, they released huge quantities of newly made viral DNA, demonstrating once again the awesome power of DNA to bring about its own replication once it gets inside a living cell.

From the 1960s to the present, hundreds of other researchers have been "playing" with DNA and RNA molecules, not only from viruses but from other living cells as well—although they would hardly consider the work they've been doing as "playing"! Among other things, they have been learning how to snip pieces of DNA out of one segment of a DNA molecule and splice them into another section where they really don't belong, just to see what will happen. They have been learning to snip whole protein-directing human DNA genes out of

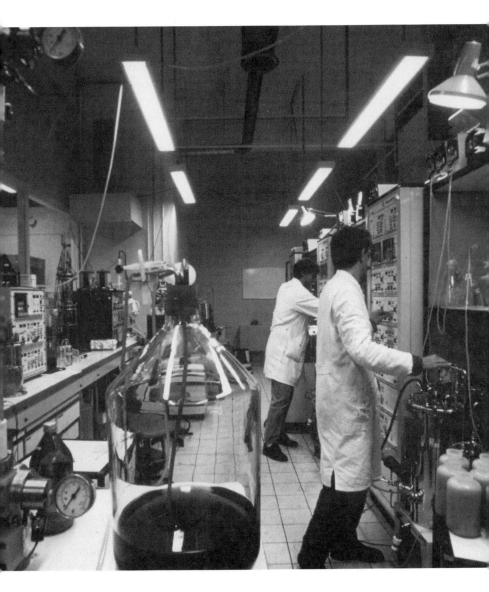

Scientists work in a fermentation laboratory where
they develop genetically engineered cultures of
bacteria, viruses, and other microorganisms used to
produce biotechnology products such as interferons.

their sequence in human cells and splice them into the DNA of living bacteria. This forces the bacteria to manufacture huge quantities of valuable human medications swiftly and very inexpensively. Those proteins would otherwise have to be extracted slowly and expensively by means of normal human protein-making processes. These techniques of so-called genetic engineering, among other things, enable us to make large quantities of valuable medicines for human use quickly and inexpensively.

In other ways, researchers are using virus DNA and RNA as tools to study the life processes going on in normal living human cells. In the chromosomes of complex cells, DNA molecules may be gathered together into thousand upon thousands of genes. Trying to sort out which specific gene with which specific structure controls which specific life function in a cell might appear to be an impossible task. But viral DNA may be made up of as few as a dozen genes, making their individual functions much easier to trace. What's more, we have seen that many viruses tend to undergo mutations through spontaneous changes in their gene arrangements. By studying the variation in function brought about by these gene changes, still more can be learned about the life-controlling power of individual genes.

With viral DNA to work with, virologists are slowly but surely stripping the enigmatic viruses of their mysteries, finding ways to take their master molecules apart and put them back together again, and observing the changes that come about as a result of these manipulations. Some scientists believe that the secret of life itself may lie in these master molecules—that their function may spell the difference between a living, reproducing cell on the one hand and an inert puddle of fluids and chemicals on the other. It would be ironic if the lowly viruses, so long considered an implacable foe of humankind, should ultimately provide us with the key to the secret of life itself!

Such basic research, teaching us more and more about what viruses are and how they cause infection, is leading in another very promising direction, too. Researchers are now targeting specific drugs that may help cure or control dangerous virus infections directly. As we have seen, zidovudine (AZT) is now in widespread use as a weapon against HIV infections. By interfering with the function of the virus's reverse transcriptase enzyme, AZT helps to block replication of the virus in the infected person. This has already begun to pay off: AIDS patients taking AZT are living longer, resisting opportunistic infections more effectively, and feeling better as a result of the drug.

Other drugs now under investigation are targeting other virus vulnerabilities. For example, in order for the AIDS virus to get inside T4 lymphocytes, it must first locate and clamp onto so-called CD4 receptor molecules on the lymphocyte surface. Researchers have been able to produce individual, separate CD4 receptor molecules. By flooding an HIV-infected person's bloodstream with these "fake" CD4 molecules, virologists hope to block all of the virus particles' receptor sites. This way, there wouldn't be any left to clamp onto the host cell receptors. Clinical testing is now under way to assess the safety and effectiveness of this possible weapon. Another drug known as ddI, also being tested, uses a still different approach to block the deadly virus's infectivity. As time goes on, more and more such drugs will be found to help fight not only HIV but other deadly viruses as well.

Viruses have been among us, playing their deadly role in human affairs, for as long as people have walked the earth. Until now they have always been invaders, enemies, destroyers of health. But today, as we learn about them for what they really are, perhaps they are destined to play a different role.

GLOSSARY

AIDS—Acquired *i*mmune *d*eficiency *s*yndrome. An ultimately fatal sexually transmitted virus infection
caused by the HIV1 (and in some parts of the world
by the HIV2) virus. Although symptoms may take
years to develop, the virus slowly destroys the function of the body's immune protective system, leads
to uncontrollable opportunistic infections, and causes
brain damage and other destructive processes in the
body.

Antigen—any foreign protein or other chemical entering
the body which the body's immune system recog-
nizes as "not-self," and therefore dangerous, and
mounts an immune reaction to destroy or immobilize.

Bacteria—single-celled plantlike microorganisms that can
enter the body and cause infection.

Chromosomes—groups of DNA or RNA molecules (see
DNA and *RNA*) which line up like beads on a string
in the nuclei of all living organisms. These molecules
provide each cell with its genetic or hereditary material to direct the size, shape, growth, and function
of daughter cells.

DNA—deoxyribonucleic acid, the great "master molecule" present in every cell in the body. This molecule contains all the genetic material necessary for guiding all gene-directed processes in the body.

Enzymes—special chemicals in the body, usually proteins, that speed up or slow down chemical reactions but do not actually take part in the reactions. They remain intact when the reaction is over.

Genes—portions of DNA molecules which, by the arrangement of amino acid bases in their molecules, carry a "code" of information that is passed on from one generation of the cell to the next.

Genetic code—all the coded information carried by a DNA molecule that directs the form, size, shape, function, and behavior of that species.

Hepatitis A—a virus that causes a dangerous infection of the liver. It is usually passed from person to person by contact with contaminated stool or feces.

Hepatitis B—another virus that causes a dangerous infection of the liver. It is usually transmitted from person to person sexually, or by contact with contaminated blood or blood products, most notably by intravenous drug users sharing dirty needles.

HIV—the human immune deficiency virus, the virus that causes AIDS.

Herpes virus—one of a family of viruses that cause a variety of different diseases in humans, most notably chicken pox, genital herpes, infectious mononucleosis, and shingles. The herpes viruses are adept at hiding away in the body and evading destruction by the body's immune protective system. The infected person carries the virus in his or her body forever, and the diseases may recur in one form or another.

Human interferon—a group of natural protein substances, manufactured by the body's white blood cells and other cells, that helps the body's immune system fight off virus infections.

Immune protective system—an organ system of the body composed of various kinds of white blood cells, proteins, antibodies, and other chemicals, that can recognize invasion of foreign "not-self" substances into the body and can then mount an attack to immobilize or destroy the invader. It is the body's first and main line of defense against life-threatening infections.

Microorganisms—any of a wide variety of bacteria, viruses, and other single-celled organisms that can find their way into the body. Some are harmless or even useful, while others can cause dangerous and deadly infections.

Nucleoproteins—molecules that combine protein portions with nucleic acid portions. DNA and RNA are forms of nucleoprotein.

Protozoans—single-celled animal-like microorganisms that can cause such diseases as malaria, amoebic dysentery, African sleeping sickness, etc.

RNA—ribonucleic acid, a form of nucleoprotein containing segments of genetic material in the cell nucleus responsible for the initiating or guiding gene-directed processes in the cell.

Yellow fever—a dangerous virus that causes a severe liver infection. Once causing thousands of deaths each year in the tropics (it is transmitted by a mosquito bite), it is now largely controlled by a very effective, long-lasting vaccine.

FOR FURTHER READING

Asimov, Isaac. *Asimov's New Guide to Science*. New York: Basic Books, 1984. (Check index for sections on *viruses*, *DNA*, and *the genetic code*.)

De Vita, Vincent, M.D., et al., editors. *AIDS*, second edition. New York: Lippincott/Harper Collins, 1989. (This is a medical textbook, but available in libraries. It is an excellent compilation of everything that is known about AIDS to publication date, from the virus itself to the social impact of the disease.)

Eron, Carol. *The Virus That Ate Cannibals*. New York: Macmillian, 1981.

Fuller, John G. *Fever! The Hunt For A New Killer Virus*. New York: Reader's Digest Press/E.P. Dutton, 1974.

Morbidity And Mortality Weekly Report (MMWR). (This is a weekly bulletin published by the Centers for Disease Control, U.S. Public Health Service, in Atlanta, Georgia. Your librarian should be able to help you locate annual index issues and individual copies. The bulletin contains accurate, up-to-date information on all kinds of virus activities all over the world.)

Nourse, Alan E. *Your Immune System*, revised edition. New York: Franklin Watts, 1989.

Patrusky, Ben. *The Search for an AIDS Vaccine*. From *Science Year* 1989. Chicago, World Book, Inc., pp. 154–168.

Rensberger, Boyce. *Creating the Ultimate Map of Our Genes*. From *Science Year* 1990. Chicago, World Book, Inc., pp. 158–171.

INDEX